Italian Americans: A Study Guide and Source Book

Alberto Meloni

San Francisco, California
1978

Published by
R&E RESEARCH ASSOCIATES, INC.
4843 Mission Street
San Francisco, California 94112
Publishers
Robert D. Reed and Adam S. Eterovich

Library of Congress Card Catalog Number

77-081035

I.S.B.N.

0-88247-482-0

Dedication

To

AGABITO MELONI

and

IRIA CAMPINI MELONI

Table of Contents

Preface

In no way is this study intended to be an original work. It is merely a compilation of the research, interpretations, and conceptualizations of numerous scholars. It is a guide and sourcebook for the study of Italian American history. It is an initial tool which should lead the student to discover for himself the vast and richer historical content of Italian Americans.

But the works in Italian American history of several scholars have been excessively influential in the writing of this survey. Indeed, at times their unexpurgated interpretations have formed the core content of individual chapters. Therefore, recognition must be given to these authors for their special contribution: Erik Amfitheatrof, Alexander De Conde, Richard Gambino, Nathan Glazer, Luciano Iorizzo, Richard Juliani, Salvatore Mondello, Daniel Moynihan, Humbert Nelli, Silvano Tomasi, and Rudolph Vecoli. If the ideas and words of these scholars and those of others have been misrepresented, I alone assume the responsibility.

Several other persons have contributed their unselfish time and efforts in the preparation of this work. My thanks must first go to a former University of Minnesota colleague Joseph Stipanovich who originally approached me with this project, and who gave frequent counsel throughout its varied stages. My deepest thanks also goes to Adam Eterovich, the Editor of R&E Research Associates, for his eternal patience and faith. But Mr. Eterovich also deserves an expression of gratitude from all students and scholars of Ethnic-Immigration history for his unselfish devotion of time, energy, and expenses to the publication of our work.

I am also indebted to my colleagues and to the History Department at Southwest Texas State University for their encouragement and goodfellowship. And, I must express a very, very special thanks to Alana for her untiring support.

But, my greatest debt is with the two Italian Americans to whom this effort is dedicated. To them, I literally owe everything.

San Marcos, Texas, 1977   A.C.M.

CHAPTER ONE: THE HISTORICAL ROOTS

I.   Introduction

After the fall of the Roman Empire, various parts of Italy were repeatedly conquered by successive waves of foreign invaders. In the Eleventh Century, the emergence of the local communes reawakened the Italian national consciousness. But national unification did not emerge again even with the coming of the Renaissance. During this period, the strong provincialism of the various city-states prohibited national unity.

Following this time of cultural, but not national rebirth, the French, the Spanish, and the Austrians reclaimed and appropriated their respective portions of Italy. The Bourbons took over the South, the Hapsburgs controlled the North, and the Papacy ruled supreme in Central Italy. But from the political ignominy endured by Italy at the Congress of Vienna in 1815, a new national movement known as the Risorgimento emerged. Its goals were liberalism and nationalism. The American and French Revolutions were its inspiration.

The revolts of the 1820s and 1830s fed more fuel to the fires of Italian nationalism. Its chief proponent, philosopher, and prophet--Giuseppe Mazzini--truly believed nationhood could be achieved through an uprising of the masses. And the mass revolt of 1848 achieved much in spirit, but very little in fact. Yet, the Kingdom of Sardinia, with its rulers in Piedmont free of any foreign domination, took interest in this burgeoning national spirt. Through the diplomacy of its Prime Minister Camillo Cavour, the rhetoric of Mazzini, and Giuseppe Garibaldi's fighting and personal charisma, the Kingdom of Sardinia enabled Italy to achieve its dream of national unification.

When Italy finally completed unification in 1870, popular opinion maintained that national unity would at last save the nation's poor, especially the peasants (contadini) of southern Italy (the Mezzogiorno). It would surely improve their desperate socio-economic condition. Unfortunately, the revolution passed the power from the foreign monarchies to the northern Italian middle class. This group was unwilling to aid the nation's peasantry in general, but it was especially prejudiced toward the southern Italian poor agricultural laborers.

For the southern peasant who had bravely fought with Garibaldi, the revolution now appeared a lost effort (revoluzione mancata). National unification marked for the poor Italian southerner another period of deprivation and frustration. This lost last hope proved to be the chief impetus for a mass exodus of southern Italians across the Atlantic to North and South America. They went searching for the socio-economic rewards denied them by their beloved peninsula.

II.   Guide and Sourcebook

Study Outline	*Notes and Sources*
A. The Italian experience in the United States can best be studied through a fourfold chronological division. The first period (1492-1870) extends from	(This is a personal division which might prove useful to the beginning student of Italian American history).

1

the initial voyages of Columbus to

the dawn of America's great industrial

revolution.

1. Navigators, explores, artists, po-   Schiavo, Italians in America Before the
   litical exiles, rich sightseers,   Civil War.
   and a few common laborers comprised
   this early immigration.

2. Sons of noble families who were   Rolle, The American Italians.
   highly educated and often multi-   (Rolle's book is quite complete in
   talented, finding few opportunities   listing the names and biographical
   at home, came to America seeking   sketches of these early Italian Ameri-
   fame, fortune, and adventure through   cans.)
   the exploration and settlement of
   a virgin continent.

3. Catholic missionaries, hoping to   (But Schiavo is still the best source,
   find both souls and riches for God,   especially for biographical sketches.)
   their Church, and perhaps them-
   selves, also came to America.

4. But prior to the Civil War, Italians   Garlick, Italy and Italians in Washing-
   made their greatest impact on Ameri-   ton's Time; Marraro, "Italian Music and
   ca in the field of the arts. Musi-   Actors."
   cians, sculptors, publishers, and
   writers came to America as the   Murdock, Constantine Brumidi.
   colonies, and later the new nation,
   increased in numbers, wealth, and
   artistic sophistication.

5. Inspired by the American and French   Scalia, "Figures of the Risorgimento in
   Revolutions, Italians attempted   America."

similar revolts to achieve nationhood. The failure of uprisings in
1821, 1830, and 1848 brought many
Italian political exiles to America,
the most memorable being Garibaldi.
Some did return to Italy during the
Risorgimento, however, many also
remained in the U.S. and became
professionals, university professors,
and leaders of the burgeoning Italian American colonies.

Goggio, "Italian Educators in Early
American Days"; Marraro, "Pioneer Italian
Teachers."

6. Even a few wealthy Italians visited
the new American nation to satisfy
their intellectual and adventurous
curiosity. And several penned their
observations and experiences.

Torrielli, Italian Opinion of America.

7. But, even during this period, Italian laborers found their way to
America. They were mostly northern
Italians with special trades and
talents desperately needed by the
new nation. However, servants,
street people, and common laborers,
though few in number, did take part
in this first but small wave of
Italian immigration to the United
States.

Rolle, The Immigrant Upraised.
(This is the only recent and scholarly
approach to discuss Italians settled
everythwere in America, but who were not
well known before the Civil War.)

B. The second period of Italian American

Foerster, The Italian Emigration.

immigration (1871-1925) resulted in the largest number of migrants from Italy going to any other single country. Likewise, it provided America with the greatest number of immigrants from any single nation.

(Though terribly outdated, this is still the best single source on Italian American history.)

1. The secondary reasons for this migration were: the desire to evade military service; the need for religious freedom (by the Waldensian Protestants); political dissatisfaction; and criminals seeking to avoid punishments or desirous of new and richer pastures.

Iorizzo and Mondello, "Origins of Italian American Criminality"; Sassone, "Italy's Criminals."

Lord, et al., _Italians in America_.

2. But the major impetus for this mass movement, also true for all Italian migration of all times, was economic.

Ratti, "Italian Migration Movements."

   a. This particular migration was actually the second great shift from Italy to the New World. The first, which occurred throughout the Nineteenth Century, went to South America, especially Argentina and Brazil.

(Foerster's book is also still the best for Italian immigration to South America.)

   b. This Italian Latin American migration was mainly composed of skilled northern Italians. Except for the volume, it resembled the Italian

immigrant flow to the U.S. prior
to 1870. But a severe outbreak of
yellow fever in Brazil, coupled
with Argentina's political, economic, and financial crises at
mid-century, brought this migration to a rapid halt.

c. By 1870, the Risorgimento had suc- Smith, Italy; A History of Sicily.
cessfully united the Peninsula
and Sicily into the Italian nation. Iorizzo and Mondello, Italian Americans.
And southern Italians, the ma- (Their book contains an excellent survey,
jority of whom had lived for and the introduction to this chapter
centuries as peansants in a quasi- heavily depended on their historical
feudalistic system, now expected perspective.)
a complete economic revolution
from the new central government
in Rome.

d. Not only did Rome fail to respond
to these southern expectations,
but it further aggravated their
condition with new, heavier, and
more unequal taxation. The old (This condition may be compared to that of
land-owning patrician class was southern Blacks once the Redeemers re-
allowed to reestablish its power gained control.)
and change the system from feudal
slavery to perpetual debt share-
cropping.

e. Nature herself added to the Boissevain, "Poverty and Politics in a

5

Study Outline	*Notes and Sources*

disappointment of southerners by inflicting phylloxera (plant lice) on their vineyards. This coupled with America's increased competition for the world's markets of the southern Italian staples-- oranges and lemons--and France's higher tariff walls against Italian wines, convinced southern Italians of the advantages of mass migration.

Sicilian Agro-Town."

(The economic depression more than the political or social hopelessness, is what ultimately drove southern Italians to migration.)

3. Thus, in the middle of the Nineteenth Century, Italian migration changed its destination from Europe and South America to the U.S. And the migrants were no longer a few skilled northern Italian artisans, but rather they were numerous southern peasants.

Ratti, "Italian Migration Movements."

Willis, Italy Chooses Europe.

4. Due to its causation, this new wave of Italian immigrants viewed their move solely as a temporary economic measure.

U.S. Immigration Commission, Reports.

a. The general desire to return to Italy, once economic independence had been achieved, was manifested by the demographic imbalances of this migration.

Foerster, "A Statistical Survey."

Study Outline	*Notes and Sources*

b. Young healthy males were the typical immigrants, with few old and fewer women arrivals. Until 1925, the number of males remained three times greater than that of females.

Livi Bacci, L'Immigrazione e L'Assimilazione. (This truly excellent statistical and demographic study is still not translated into English. But the universality of numbers makes it easy enough to understand.)

c. These immigrants possessed high illiteracy rates and lacked the skills necessary for decent and profitable labor in a growing industrial society.

Erikson, American Industry.

d. With the instability of family life, committed to return to Italy, and relegated to the lowest rung in a new and alien society, this new migration encountered difficulties unknown by earlier immigrants.

Tomasi, L., The Italian American Family.

Chapin, Standard of Living.

5. This flood of southern Italian young male peasants who were unskilled, illiterate, and temporary migrants abetted the rise of a renascent American nativism.

La Gumina, Wop. (This volume of documentary sources, affirming the discrimination against Italian Americans, is both captivating and quite scholarly.)

6. The response of the American government to this nativist agitation was to enact strict immigration restriction.

Higham, Strangers in the Land.

C. The third period of Italian American

Castiglione, "Italian Immigration";

Study Outline	*Notes and Sources*
immigration (1926-1945) was characterized by decreased numbers arriving to the U.S. But, it was during this time that increased participation, integration, and assimilation of Italians into American society took place. These years also introduced in the Italian American community a consciousness of national identity, purpose, and leadership.	Dore, "Some Social and Historical Aspects." (Greater details on this period can be found in later chapters.) Lombardo, The Italians in America.
D. The fourth and final period of Italian American immigration (1946-Present) has been marked by small numbers of migrants coming to the U.S. However, during this time, many third and fourth generation Italian Americans have fully assimilated, if not yet totally Americanized. This process has caused tensions with the earlier generations. The arrival of new and different ethnic groups has caused tensions for the rising aspirations of the assimilated Italian Americans. And the recent celebrations of ethnicity and the glorification of a peoples' roots have confronted the young American Italian with perplexing questions of identity.	Monticelli, "Italian Emigration." Grossman, The Italians in America. (Again, since much of this is discussed in detail in later chapters, only a brief analysis is presented here.) Child, Italian or American. Bayor, "Italians, Jews, and Ethnic Conflict."

8

Study Outline	*Notes and Sources*
1. As a result of the still-enforced limiting quotas, it is only close relatives of Italian Americans who can migrate to the U.S. with little difficulty.	Velikonja, "Italian Immigrants."
2. A rather large number of northern and southern Italian "specialists" have migrated to the U.S. since W.W.II under "specialist visas." This quota, a program of America's "brain drain" of the world's foreign talent, has received special and unlimited preferences.	Tomasi, "Italian Immigration." Fleming and Bailyn, Intellectual Migrations.
3. But many Italians are once again migrating to northern Europe, to Australia, and to South America rather than waiting endlessly for a visa to the U.S. Furthermore, the greater economic opportunities, still the Italians' chief reason for migration, appear to be present in greater quantities in other parts of the world than in present-day North America.	Willis, Italy Chooses Europe. (Many nations, such as Switzerland and Australia, have received so many Italians that they too are instituting limiting racial quotas.)

III. Conclusion

If economics has been the primary and eternal motive inspiring, urging, and forcing the Italians perpetually to migrate throughout the globe, then--detailed attention should be given to the economics of the Italian American experience.

CHAPTER TWO: THE ECONOMICS OF MIGRATION

I. Introduction

In recent years, the United States Bureau of the Census has found the median income of Italian Americans to be slightly higher than the average income of the total U.S. population. Yet, the percentage of Italian Americans in white collar work is still lower than for most other ethnic groups. Indeed, in several U.S. cities even more Blacks are employed as professionals than Italians.

The occupational history of Italian Americans has always been characterized by ever so slight changes. As many as two-thirds of the second generation have remained common laborers like their fathers. The gap between the first and second generations in occupation and income is still smaller for Italian Americans than for any other major European ethnic group in America. It is true, however, that these economic differences are widening between the second and third generations.

As late as the Thirties and Forties, the few Italian American professionals were chosen from among the small group of northern Italians or from the few non-peasant southerners. Today, the grandchildren of numerous southern Italian peasant immigrants to America are at last moving into the professions. But, it is still predominantly in the television industry, in newspaper reporting, and in sports that their talents have been found highly useful. The climb up the corporate ladder to the very pinnacle, however, is still only a professional dream for most Italian Americans.

It should also be remembered that today many Italian Americans have risen in status and social mobility not necessarily because they have at last received their commensurate rewards within the American economy, but because Blacks, Hispanic-Americans, and Indians have in many American cities replaced Italians at the bottom of the economic ladder.

Unfortunately, Italian Americans have never solidly united into an ethnic labor movement and agitated for their just economic rewards. Due to the psychological and spiritual scars bequeathed them by their peasant history, they have always been more interested in daily personal and familial survival. In a society distinguished for its fierce competition at all levels, but especially in economics, this concentration upon mere survival of the self has generally cost the Italian Americans the easier and quicker realization of the American dream.

II. Guide and Sourcebook

Study Outline	*Notes and Sources*
A. For the most part, the principal reason for Italian immigration to the U.S. has always been economic. Italians have generally come to America with the hope of improving their	(This generalization has been proven accurate so many times that it is generally accepted by all sources.)

Study Outline	*Notes and Sources*

economic outlook.

1. Before 1870, besides navigators, explorers, and adventurers, Italy did contribute numerous common laborers to the American community.

Schiavo, Italian American History; Van Doren and Moquin, A Documentary History.

   a. These were predominantly northern Italians. Many migrated with their entire household. And most were skilled artisans.

Iorizzo and Mondello, The Italian Americans.

   b. Because of the journey's hardships, length, and cost, this migration became largely a permanent one.

Lopreato, Italian Americans.

   c. Permanence is further evidenced by their equal choices for settlement of interior as well as coastal areas of the U.S.

Meade, "Italians on the Land." Rolle, The Immigrant Upraised. (It is too often forgotten that Italians also settled the interior farm lands.)

2. While retaining the same economic motivations, the nature of Italian immigration to the U.S. changed markedly after 1870.

U.S. Immigration Commission, Reports, 1911.

   a. These newcomers were predominantly southern Italians. Many were healthy single males. And most were illiterate, unskilled, peasant laborers.

Schuyler, "Italian Immigration"; Stella, Some Aspects of Italian Immigration.

   b. They viewed their American sojourn as temporary. Their only hope and desire were to return wealthier to their native Italian village in order to purchase either land or a higher social status.

c. Fortunately, their arrival coincided with America's greatest need for cheap unskilled labor in factories, on railroads, in mines, on farms, and in steel plants.

Sheridan, "Italian, Slavic, and Hungarian Unskilled Immigrants."

d. But these large numbers of new foreign workers also aroused America's nativistic fears due to their high rate of repatriation, their use of the Padrone System, and their alleged radicalism.

Higham, Strangers in the Land.

(La Gumina's Wop contains excellent examples of this nativism.)

3. From 1926 to 1945, with the number of new arrivals severely limited by U.S. legislated restrictions and by War, Italians managed to exert their concerted energies and powers for increased economic stability and upward mobility within American society.

Kessner, The Golden Door.

Ianni, "Residential and Occupational Mobility."

a. They increased their numbers among blue collar workers.

b. When tenement and children's work became restricted, women made headway into the clothing factories. Some of these Italian American

Odencrantz, Italian Women in Industry; Seidman, The Needle Trades.

12

Study Outline	*Notes and Sources*

women were even accepted as cleri-
cal and sales clerks.

c. Politics and crime, especially
during Prohibition, provided new
avenues for greater fortunes and
status.

Nelli, <u>Business of Crime</u>.

d. But several factors still miti-
gated against full and equal economic advancement for Italian
Americans.

Glazer and Moynihan, <u>Beyond the Melting
Pot</u>.

   1) The new immigrants' previous experiences had not properly
equipped them for the ever increasing skills demanded by
the ever emerging technology.

(Most of these new immigrants, it will be
remembered, were southern Italian
peasants.)

   2) These new immigrants did not believe in the necessity or value
of formal education. Most of
their new generations had been
and still were happy to follow
in their fathers' economic foot-
steps.

(Formal education was frowned upon in
most Italian American families until recent times.)

   3) Their desire for security was
far greater than their desire
for a higher economic status.
This voluntarily tied them to
the same job for a lifetime.

(Security could be assured, if the Italian
American, having found a job, held on to
it, and passed it on to his son.)

4. Since the Second World War, the

Velikonja, "Italian Americans."

13

number of Italians coming to the
U.S. has remained relatively small
and stable.

a. Only a few restless southern   Monticelli, "Italian Immigration."
    Italian peasants continue to
    migrate to the U.S. And due to
    America's still existant quotas,
    limiting the number of Italians
    coming to the U.S., most of these
    new immigrants are relatives of
    Italian American citizens.

b. Some northern and southern Italian   Fermi, Illustrious Immigrants; Fleming
    specialists in the arts and the   and Bailyn, Intellectual Migration.
    sciences have migrated during the
    post-War American "brain drain" of
    the world's economically weaker
    nations.

c. Many Italians are once again mi-   Willis, Italy Chooses Europe.
    grating to Northern Europe, South
    Africa, Australia, and South
    America rather than to the U.S.

d. The Third and Fourth Generations   Glazer and Moynihan, Beyond the Melting
    have obtained greater opportuni-   Pot.
    ties in business and the profes-   (Many of the concepts presented in this
    sions. This is especially due to   chapter's introduction are a product of
    the growth of government bureauc-   this enduring book.)
    racy and the expanding white collar
    job market.

Study Outline	Notes and Sources

B. During the years 1870 to 1925, Italian American immigration developed an unusually high rate of repatriation.

Caroli, _Italian Repatriation_; Gilkey, "The U.S. and Italy."

1. American nativists became indignant over the Italians' tendency to migrate solely for seasonal labor, to reap personal wealth, and to return home at the first best opportunity.

2. Nativist societies such as the American Protective Association, the most powerful and most vicious, disparagingly dubbed these migrants the "birds of passage." And, they persisted in attempts to limit their numbers, their employment, and their savings.

(The Caroli work is the best source in English for the study of repatriation.)

3. However, America desperately needed this source of cheap common labor, and for several advantageous reasons, even the Italian government encouraged this temporary migration.

Douglas, _Influence of the Southern Italian_; Tosti, "Italy's Attitude."

a. It provided a "safety-valve" for Italy's increasing unemployment.

b. Between what the immigrants mailed to Italian banks and what they personally brought back, this migration made Italy much wealthier.

(Immigrant banks were very haphazardly organized institutions. They were more than not begun by an individual with a stronger desire to relieve the immigrant of his earnings, rather than protect

c. It considerably aided Italy's

Study Outline	*Notes and Sources*

burgeoning shipping industry.

d. And largely as a result of the rising demand for Italian products by her immigrants abroad, Italy was able to solve her unfavorable balance of trade.

4. The largest number of Italian arrivals to and repatriates from the U.S. occurred between 1900 and 1914.

   a. About three million Italians came to the U.S. during this time, and one-half that number returned to Italy.

   b. By 1914, one out of every twenty Italians had been to America at least once. Most had made several trips.

   c. The seasonal and temporary nature of this migration is evidenced by the peak of arrivals occurring in March through June, while the largest repatriation took place from October to December.

5. This temporary migration had some beneficial as well as some undesirable affects upon Italian society.

   a. Repatriates introduced into Italy a better habit of hygiene.

Notes and Sources:

them. Yet, one of America's great bankers, Amedeo Giannini, and one of America's great banks, the Bank of America, have risen from such humble origins as immigrant banks.)

James and James, Biography of a Bank.

(See Appendix for the statistical details.)

(The author's paternal grandfather made eighteen trips to the U.S., never twice to the same city.)

Cerase, "A Study of Italian Migrants."

16

b. They made Italians more appreciative of formal education.

c. Returning Italians were more aware of civic responsibilities as well as opportunities.

d. Italian criminality decreased since migration alleviated some of Italy's unemployed, who might have otherwise swelled the criminal ranks.

Foerster, <u>Italian Emigration</u>; Sassone, "Italy's Criminals."

e. But, this returning migration also introduced high levels of tuberculosis throughout Italy.

Cerase, "Expectations and Reality."

f. And, the returning Italians also brought back an increased propensity for excesses in drinking and gambling.

C. In 1901 the U.S. Industrial Commission erroneously identified the chief cause for the increase of Italian unskilled laborers in America to be the existance of the "Padrone System."

Koren, "The Padrone System"; Lipari, "The Padrone System."

1. A formal "contract-labor system," whereby American employers hired workers in foreign countries to provide cheap unskilled labor in America, existed until 1885 when the U.S. Congress outlawed it.

Iorizzo and Mondello, <u>Italian Americans</u>.

Study Outline	_Notes and Sources_

2. Many Italian American immigrants, permanently settled in the U.S. and already prosperous, decided to fill the resultant void in America's cheap labor needs and demands. They became labor agents who surreptitiously contracted their fellow countrymen for American employers.

3. With the promise of lucrative employment, these agents encouraged many poor Italian peasants to immigrate. The latter paid an initial fee to the agent, and promised a periodic commission from future wages.

    Nelli, "The Italian Padrone System."

4. In many instances, the agent did indeed become the workers' boss or owner (padrone), since the American employer often issued all instructions, payments, or reprimands solely through the Padrone.

    (Nelli's article is the definitive study, thus far, on the Padrone System. Much of this treatment comes from his work.)

5. The amount of commission (bossatura) paid by the immigrant depended on the length of employment, amount of wages, and the additional services such as shelter, food, and counsel which the Padrone provided.

6. Obvious inherent evils existed within
    such a system.

    a. By charging exorbitant commissions,
        especially for food and shelter,
        the Padrone could keep an immigrant
        in his perpetual debt.

    b. The Padrone might hire and fire at
        will depending on his need for
        greater initial fees and higher
        "bossature."

    c. The Padrone might not provide all
        the services paid for by his work-
        ers. And the quality of those
        services rendered might be in-
        ferior to what could be purchased
        cheaper within the open society.

    d. The "Padrone Camps" connected with
        railroad and farm labor, in which
        the workers were totally dependent
        upon their agent, were often no
        better than "slave-owner" societal
        frameworks and relationships.

7. Yet, several advantages and benefits   Iorizzo, "The Padrone and Immigrant Dis-
    of the Padrone System have been too   tribution."
    often overlooked.

    a. The Padrone brought together
        American capital and Italian labor
        at those times when both were in

19

the greatest need of each other.

b. The Padrone provided the immigrant
    workers with services not easily
    found or offered within the larger
    American community.

c. The Padrone, when necessary, often
    mediated successfully between immi-
    grant workers and their American
    employers.

8. The Padrone System thrived during
    the decades of the 1880s and 90s.
    Afterwards, it steadily declined.

a. After 1904, social workers con-
    vinced numerous state governments
    to outlaw the System.

b. Most Italians arriving in the U.S.   Nelli, Italians in Chicago.
    after 1890 usually came to join
    relatives who, already having ex-
    perienced and extricated them-
    selves from the System, did not
    allow these newcomers to fall prey
    to it.

D. The arrival of this "new" Italian immi-   Meltzer, Bread and Roses; Preston,
    gration to the U.S. aroused an addi-   Aliens and Dissenters.
    tional fear within American nativists.
    They envisioned these illiterate
    peasant masses becoming Anarchists
    and Socialists thereby giving rise

to labor and social radicalism.

1. Before 1870, some northern Italian immigrants to the U.S. had joined trade unions. They had known similar associations both in Italy and in their earlier travels throughout northern Europe.

   Baily, "Italians and Organized Labor."

2. But such organizations were completely alien to the masses of southern Italian peasants who arrived in America after 1870.

   Baily, "Italians and the Development of Organized Labor."

3. These migrants were more interested in practical labor-related grievances than they were in philosophical or intellectual economic considerations.

4. The key factor in organizing these new arrivals was "bargaining power." This was a union's assurance that it could achieve its goals of higher wages and better working conditions. When such assurances existed, Italians organized quickly and most effectively.

   Fenton, "Italians in the Labor Movement."
   (As is often the case, this work by Fenton remains the best source on the subject.)

5. Radicals, Socialists, and Anarchists could rarely provide such assurances, hence, the small active membership of the Italian American

   Rosemblum, Immigrant Workers.

working masses in their organizations.

6. Yet, American nativists insisted on
viewing Italian Americans as labor
and social radicals. And in several
instances, they had good reasons to
do so.

   a. In 1912, the predominantly Sici-
       lian millworkers in Lawrence,
       Massachusetts not only struck, but
       also accepted the radical leader-
       ship of the I.W.W.--International
       Workers of the World, a militantly
       anticapitalist union.

   b. In 1913, Anarchists led Italian
       textile workers in a violent strike
       in Paterson, New Jersey.

   c. In 1921, the trial of Nicola Sacco
       and Bartolomeo Vanzetti in Dedham,
       Massachusetts came to symbolize
       the threat of Italian American
       radicalism. These two adherents
       of Anarchism were convicted and
       executed for a dubious crime based
       on dubious evidence through dubi-
       ous justice.

7. But, Italian Americans may have always been more concerned with the

---

Higham, Strangers in the Land.

Amfitheatrof, The Children of Columbus;
Cole, Immigrant City.

Joughin and Morgan, The Legacy of Sacco
and Vanzetti; Russell, Tragedy in Dedham.

Ehrman, The Case That Will Not Die.
(It is still hotly debated in the
Massachusetts Legislature to this very
day.)

(This paragraph and the one following con-
sist of strictly personal observations

22

practical economic gains of revolt and not with the philosophical and drastic societal alterations of revolution. They may have been activists only on those occasions when America withheld from them a share of its capitalist wealth and not from any desire to overthrow the capitalist system itself.

formed in the course of formal study and personal experiences.)

8. Frequently, Italian Americans were not only feared by the ruling establishment for their radicalism, but they were hated equally as much by the proletariat for their conservatism.

   a. The latter did not want Italians to accept sub-standard wages.

   b. As a result, American employers often used Italians as threats to organized labor. More from ignorance than from willful intent, Italians allowed themselves to be used as strikebreakers or "scabs."

De Conde, *Half Bitter, Half Sweet*.

Rosemblum, *Immigrant Workers*.

   c. Many unions refused admittance to Italians willing to join for no other reason than racial prejudice.

9. For various reasons Italian immigrant laborers were able to organize much

Baily, "The Italian and the Development of Organized Labor."

more quickly and effectively in

other Western Hemisphere countries

such as Argentina than in the U.S.

a. Italians unfortunately arrived in
    great numbers in the U.S. after
    labor had already begun to organ-
    ize. Consequently, they were un-
    able to exert any decisive leader-
    ship influences which might have
    inclined the masses of Italian
    workers to join the unions.

b. Too many Italians were arriving in
    America too fast, hence, they be-
    came too visible. This caused
    normal apprehensions within the
    establishment as well as within
    the labor unions.

c. And even the northern Italian
    Americans, some of whom had al-
    ready organized, refused to aid
    their southern countrymen due to
    Italian national prejudices.

d. In America, craft unions were too
    exclusive and job oriented. Ital-
    ians needed services better pro-
    vided by other organizations.

e. And finally ,the cultural barriers
    for Italians such as language and

(Much of this section is taken from
Baily's own research.)

(Baily's article is quite definitive
on the subject.)

religion were much greater in the U.S. than in any other country in the Western Hemisphere.

10. What radicalism did exist among Italian Americans ultimately failed for several historical reasons.

Murray, Red Scare.

   a. W.W. I made strikes appear treasonous.

   b. What little Italian leadership did exist in the I.W.W. left in disgust after 1917 due to policy disagreements.

   c. After W.W.I there occurred an anti-Red hysteria which sought out and deported many Italian radical leaders.

   d. The hopes of the Bolshevik Revolution turned into the nightmares of the Stalinist era.

   e. The New Deal gave hope for better working and living conditions for America's common laborers.

   f. And by W.W. II, the hatred of American capitalism had been replaced among the radicals by the more widely accepted fear of Soviet Communism and Italian Fascism.

(De Conde has an excellent treatment in his study on this very subject. In fact, assessed in its totality, De Conde's book is probably the best single work on Italian Americans since Foerster. But unfortunately De Conde does not treat

Latin America or any statistical surveys.)

III. Conclusion

In spite of the large number of repatriations, for the most part, over the entirety of Italian American history, the immigrants did permanently settle in the U.S. Once this decision of permanency had been made, the Italian American began constructing his new social and cultural milieu, based it upon the culture and the society he had known in Italy. And much of the Italian Americans' pains, sufferings, and despairs derived from this confrontation of their "Cultural Baggage" with the American host society and its alien, as well as ever changing, cultural patterns.

CHAPTER THREE: SOCIETY AND CULTURE

I. Introduction

The Italians, like all other immigrant peoples who have come to America, also brought with them a "cultural baggage" which greatly determined the results of their confrontation with American society. The outcome of this conflict usually depended upon the extent to which the principal features of the immigrants' culture could survive transplantation. And Italian culture has always been most difficult to transplant. But it proved to be especially so when reaching American shores. This difficulty emanated both from the unique characteristics of Italian culture, as well as from the evolving cultural patterns of the American host society. And Italians found it most painful, even if willing, to adapt.

For numerous reasons Italian culture has always been most difficult to transplant. It is poor in articulate content. It has lacked a common language and tradition. And no institutional framework has ever really been integral to it. But the particular culture of the Italian peasant, from whose ranks the greatest numbers of Italian American immigrants have come, had even more severe difficulties in transplantation. It was deeply rooted in the soil. It rested mainly on oral tradition. It accorded great dignity to manual skills. It took religion for granted. And it contained no element of community participation or social organization beyond the immediate family circle.

The only institution of any real significance in Italian culture was the family. Often, that was the totality of Italian peasant culture. Everything revolved about it. If that institution faltered, Italian culture often had no other basis of support. The Italian people, especially the peasants, made family and culture inseparable.

But America's societal, economic, and cultural pressures quickly unmasked the Italian facade of cultural unity based on the family. The Italians confronted an American society which, responding to technological, political, social, and economic changes, especially after each of the two World Wars, altered the traditional American view of the family. Perhaps, but they were most certainly at odds when the greatest numbers of Italians first reached America. Thus, Italian family-based-culture was not able to transplant itself successfully. Nor were the Italians capable of easily adopting the new American culture, which no longer possessed the family as its essential centerpiece.

II. Guide and Sourcebook

Study Outline	*Notes and Sources*
A. For the majority of Italians, and especially for the southern peasants who migrated to the U.S., there existed one and only one social reality-- the family.	Gambino, Blood of My Blood. (Many of the concepts in this chapter are derived from Gambino's excellent work.)

Study Outline	*Notes and Sources*
1. The relation and attitudes of Italians toward society were exclusively regulated by an all-encompassing set of rules.	Williams, South Italian Folkways.
2. This cultural and behavioral system has been called "l'ordine della famiglia," which literally means "the order of the family."	(This is Gambino's terminology as he describes his own Italian American childhood in New York.)
3. According to this system, one owes absolutely nothing to anyone outside the immediate family circle. And each individual's life efforts should be exclusively directed to advance the interests of his family.	Dore, "Social and Historical Aspects of Italian Immigration."
4. Sociologists have referred to this system as "amoral familism."	Banfield, Moral Basis of a Backward Society.
5. The system also contained an understood and accepted hierarchy which determined all social interaction.	
a. Uppermost in an individual's total considerations, at all times and in every circumstance, was the honor and welfare of his immediate family.	
b. The "compari" or "padrini" were next in importance. The female counterparts were "commare" and "madrine." They could be extended family members, intimate friends,	(Usually, the padrino and madrina were a child's baptismal godparents.)

or venerated elders.

c. Next in order came those friends
to whom one only occasionally
spoke in friendly terms.

d. The "stranieri" or strangers were
the last in social importance.
This category included everyone
else in society. One had only
absolutely necessary contact with
them. This group could also be
used by an individual to any purpose for the advancement of his
family's interest.

(Gambino in his book describes this
hierarchy quite vividly.)

6. The family was the chief preserver
and transmitter of "la via vecchia"
or traditional lifestyles.

Gans, _Urban Villagers_.

7. All persons or institutions which
aided in this preservation and
transmittal were tolerated. Those
which stood in the way were not.

8. "La via vecchia" contained numerous
and stringent axioms.

Campisi, "Ethnic Family Patterns."

a. The family is supreme. It must be
patriarchal, well integrated,
stationary, and possess all goals
in common. The individual always
subordinates himself to the family.

b. The father maintains the highest

(Campisi's article handily diagrams

Study Outline	Notes and Sources

Study Outline

status in the family. He is re-
spected, imitated, and greatly
loved. Through and with his
family the father also attains
the respect of the community.

c. The mother is the center of do-
mestic life.

d. Children are an economic asset.
They must live exclusively for
the parents and the family.

e. Sons must work to contribute to
the support of the family. They
are superior to the daughters.
Girls are educated only for marriage. And it is the eldest son
who inherits the father's status
within the family.

f. Marriage comes early in life with
a mate from the same Italian village, and one selected by the
parents. Premarital sex is taboo
at least until after the engage-
ment.

g. The family should be large. No
birth control, divorce, adultery,
separation, or disertion are
tolerated.

h. All culture and behavioral norms

Notes and Sources

Italian American family patterns as they
evolved over the first four generations.)

Gebhart, Growth and Development of
Italian Children.

Cordasco and Bucchioni, "Italian Social
Backgrounds."

Williams, South Italian Folkways.

Rosenwaike, "Two Generations: Their
Fertility."

Study Outline	*Notes and Sources*

are transmitted through the family.

B. On arrival in the U.S., most Italians
    tended to congregate in those urban
    neighborhoods inhabited by individuals
    from their own particular Italian
    village. They knew each other as
    "paesani" or neighbors from the same
    town.

1. This aggregation was another means
    of preserving "la via vecchia" in
    spite of migration to a foreign land.

2. Due to this peculiar associational
    tendency, which has been called the
    "paesani principle," Italian immi-
    grants did not establish a single
    monolithic community. Rather, they
    created a series of individualized
    "Little Italys" scattered throughout
    the urban centers of America.

3. Beyond a general societal cleavage
    between the residents of northern
    and southern regions, Italians in
    America separated even according to
    individual Italian villages. This
    attitude and behavior is known as
    "campanilismo." It is the refusal
    to concern oneself or deal with any-
    one or anything beyond one's village

Gans , Urban Villagers.

Mangano, Italian Colonies.

Ernst, Immigrant Life in New York.

Stella, Effects of Urban Congestion.

Juliani, "Origin and Development of the
Italian Community."
(The concept of the "paesani principle
and its consequences belong to Juliani.)

Pileggi, "Little Italy."

Vecoli, "Contadini in Chicago."

church steeple.

4. Since most residents in American "Little Italys" usually came from the same Italian region, the inhabitants would further segregate themselves on a particular block according to village or even according to dialect.

      Nelli, Italians in Chicago.

      (To Nelli, the debt is also great for many of the concepts and much of the information contained in this chapter.)

5. Italian immigrants did gain certain advantages both from the "paesani principle" and from "campanilismo."

      Nelli, "Italians in Urban America."

  a. They initiated and maintained the "chain-migration" basis for most of the Italian American immigration process.

      (Much of what follows is again from the previously noted Juliani article.)

  b. They provided immigrants with information, money, and encouragement for migration.

  c. On the immigrants' arrival, they offered physical safety and the means of survival such as work, shelter, and friendships.

  d. But most important, they gave the immigrants the time necessary to adjust successfully to an alien society without demanding an immediate and complete break with the familiar past.

      Bianco, The Two Rosetos.

6. Yet, both the "paesani principle" and "campanilismo" did cause serious problems for Italian American immigrants.

   a. They prevented Italian Americans from quickly unifying in order to exert political pressures for social and economic betterment.

   b. They did somewhat retard the Italians' adjustment to American society and values.

                                  Child, <u>Italian or American</u>.

7. But adjustment inevitably did occur. And for several reasons, it took place among the Italians even more quickly than for many other immigrant groups in America.

                                  Asciolla, <u>Contributions of Italian Americans</u>.

   a. Italians did not remain long in any one dwelling within the "Little Italys." But they also did not long remain within these strictly Italian enclaves.

                                  Nelli, <u>Italians in Chicago</u>. (Nelli presents much statistical data to prove this very assertion.)

   b. Their incessant desire to own property, and especially their own home, was a constant drive toward integration within the larger American community.

                                  Douglas, <u>Influence of the Southern Italian</u>.

   c. In America, the necessities of survival such as making a living,

                                  Wheeler, <u>The Immigrant Experience</u>.

finding a wife, owning a home, and
raising children tended to unite
Italians irregardless of previous
regional, provincial, village, or
dialect associations.

d. Soon Italian Americans came to
recognize themselves as a national
ethnic group. This provided them
with the necessary social, cultural, and political confidence
and leverage within American society. "Paesani" came to mean
fellow Italians in America rather
than fellow villagers.

Ware, Greenwich Village.
(Recognition must be given to Ware for
the ideas which comprise this chapter's
introduction.)

e. This national identity took place
among Italians in America as early
as the 1920s and 30s, while in
Italy it is still today only an
aspired goal.

Mariano, Second Generation.

C. Perhaps, the greatest cost to Italian
Americans for their adherence to "la
via vecchia" was their painfully slow
social and economic upward mobility.
This principally resulted from the
lack of emphasis upon formal education for their young.

U.S. Immigration Commission, Children
of Immigrants, 1911.

1. To be educated in an Italian family
meant learning and following the

Covello, Social Background of the Italo-
American School Child.

Study Outline	*Notes and Sources*

dictums of the "old ways" rather

than receiving formal instruction.

2. Intellectual curiosity and original-
   ity were viewed as possible threats
   to the continuation of "la via
   vecchia."

   Covello, "High School and Its Immigrant
   Community."

3. Italians, unlike many other immigrant groups, did not for a long
   time take advantage of America's
   public school system, which was the
   most common channel to economic
   success.

   Cordasco, "The Children of Immigrants
   in the Schools."

4. Within two generations after 1890,
   this attitude among Italian Americans changed, as did much of their
   adherence to "la via vecchia." Yet,
   to this day, Italian Americans who
   do seek education still do not for
   the most part gravitate toward
   speculative studies. Rather, they
   seek the practical sciences which
   will prepare them for greater living
   and status achieving professions.

   Carpenter, Immigrants and Their Children;
   Corsi, "Italian Immigrants and Their
   Children"; Glazer and Moynihan, Beyond
   the Melting Pot; Hutchinson, Immigrants
   and Their Children.

III. Conclusion

   Within American society the Italian was unable to maintain his cultural unity
through the central institutional framework of the family. As the little transplanted
Italian culture gave way with the disintegration of family life, the Italian American
began his search for alternative institutions which might aid him to reestablish the
social and cultural milieu so necessary for survival in an alien land. Though he was
not overly fond of formal religion in Italy, the Italian American, having lost the

cultural anchor of the family, at first turned to the Catholic Church for possible help and solace.

CHAPTER FOUR: THE IMMIGRANT CHURCH

I. Introduction

The principal question faced by the American Catholic Church with regard to immigration has been whether or not the Catholic immigrants have kept their faith during and after the process of transplantation. For the most part, both the Church hierarchy and the Church's many historians have unwaveringly answered in the affirmative. The American Catholic Church has pictured itself as meeting and surmounting the challenge of assimilating the nation's polyglot immigrant masses. Indeed, for the Church and its apologists immigration has not at all been a difficult problem to surmount, but rather a fortunate occurrence which has produced a phenomenal growth of U.S. Catholicism.

But beyond keeping the immigrants faithful, American Catholicism sees itself as having fulfilled a second vital function. This is its contribution toward fashioning the immigrant into a good American citizen. The Church, whose origins and leadership are derived from a foreign capitol, ever mindful that its American patriotism is perpetually suspect, decided to become the central means through which Catholic immigrants might reach total Americanization. Furthermore, as a conservative influence, the Church seized the opportunity to check the spread of the radical labor, political, and societal tendencies especially prevalent with the Catholic southern European immigrants to America. Through them, the Church saw its chance to contribute stability to the American social order and solid citizens to the American nation.

The Italian American immigrants, however, became a special case. Soon after their numerous arrivals to America during 1880 and 1890, their presence within the American Catholic Church became known as the "Italian Problem." The American Church saw the southern Italian peasants as indifferent toward religion. It interpreted their Catholicism as primitive, medieval, and irreligious. For its efforts to properly instruct them, the Church witnessed many Italian Americans joining Protestant churches. And those Italian Americans who remained nominal Catholics soon began to fall away from active participation in formal religious services.

In her attempt to solve this "Italian Problem," the American Catholic Church confronted the difficulties spawned by her efforts to combine various world Catholic traditions into one American Church. And the controversies over her self-assigned role to be an agent of Americanization also became evident. Meanwhile, the Church received the deserved indictment of unresponsiveness to the needs of the nation's poor, disadvantaged, and exploited foreign population.

A study of the "Italian Problem" within the history of American Catholicism, more than attention upon any other group, should test the validity of the Church's assimilation thesis. Did the Church truly integrate the immigrants into American society? Or did its own ethnic and American foundations make it difficult to absorb different cultural backgrounds and religious practices? And how has the Church survived the seemingly inevitable creation of today's American immigrant social, cultural, political, and religious mosaic? Some clues to the possible answers should be discovered in a brief survey of the American Catholic Church's "Italian Problem."

II. Guide and Sourcebook

Study Outline	*Notes and Sources*

A. Catholic missionaries, many of Italian descent traveled to the New World with the early French and Spanish explorers.

Rolle, American Italians.

1. Many of these clerics were Franciscan and Jesuit priests. While the explorers and adventurers searched for gold, these dedicated servants of God sought to mine souls from among the various Indian people.

Rolle, Immigrant Upraised.
(Both of Rolle's books are excellent for detailed accounts of these early missionary explorers.)

2. But often, these missionaries were themselves more interested in worldly possessions than in the eternal souls. Some left Italy not always by choice due to their irreligious behavior. In America, they contributed to exploration and early settlement. And quite a number lost their lives in these pursuits of riches, conversions, and settlement.

Schiavo, Italians Before the Civil War.

3. In time, as a fledgling Italian American population emerged, some members of the Italian clergy, often from among the Orders, voluntarily came to America to bring religious faith and solace to these immigrants. Most established missions and churches in the urban centers along

Schiavo, Four Centuries.
(The second volume is a detailed account of early efforts by the Catholic Church among the Italians in America.)

Femminella, "The Impact of Italian Migration."

the East and West coasts of America
where much of this early Italian immigration also found its economic
livelihood.

4. In 1848 numerous Italian Jesuits,
exiled for their part in the revolt,
came to America. These highly educated clerics became professors of
languages, sciences, history, ethics,
and cannon law at various American
universities.

(Once again, Rolle and Schiavo are un-
equaled in their treatment of the subject.)

5. In the 1850s, when Garibaldi exiled
the Jesuits from Sicily, once again
many came to America. Some con-
tinued to enter the teaching professions. But many now began to
serve a growing Italian American
population, especially in the Great
Northwest. A few of these Jesuits,
as part of their services within
Italian American congregations,
also contributed to the American
political, social, and economic
general welfare.

Iorizzo and Mondello, Italian Americans.

B. After 1870, when Italians reached
America in unprecedented numbers, the
American Catholic Church faced the
problem of incorporating these new

Trisco, The Holy See.

arrivals into its existing institutional structures. The difficulties which the Church encountered with the Italians in the years 1870 to 1925 led to discussions of the Church's role and affect within the American immigration process.

Browne, "The Italian Problem in the Catholic Church."

1. When the large numbers of Italians first came to America, it was the Irish who primarily dominated the American Catholic Church.

Schiavo, Italian American History.

   a. For the Irish Americans the Catholic Church was integral to their nationalism.

   b. But for the Italian, especially the southern peasant, the Church was the enemy of his liberty and progress. It was the Church which had maintained a stranglehold on central Italy through its Papal States thereby retarding Italian national unification. And it was also the Church which, after the victory of the Risorgimento, sided with the northern Italian middle class, and conspired to deny the Italian peasants in the South their hard-earned social and political

Vecoli, "Prelates and Peasants." (Vecoli's article is still the best on the subject. The introduction to this chapter owes much to his study.)

rewards of the revolution.

c. Beyond viewing Catholicism through   Vecoli, "Contadini in Chicago."
    this political prism, the southern
    Italian peasant , for whom life was
    usually a hopeless , fatalistic, and
    miserable undertaking, fashioned
    his Catholic faith from a series of
    evil eyes (malocchio) , curses,
    potions, charms , and magic. The
    "contadini" found their patron
    saints, village priests , and local
    sourcerers (mago and strega) much
    more meaningful and reliable for
    solving daily problems. Besides,
    in the "Mezzogiorno" it was not the
    Church but the family which estab-
    lished and influenced the moral
    values of one's life.

d. The southern Italian peasant was   Russo, "Three Generations."
    a nominal Roman Catholic who pre-
    served many characteristics of
    pagan civilizations.

e. Italian intellectuals were gener-
    ally anti-clerical (mangiapreti).
    And they often extracted support
    for their hatred from the rightful
    political and social indignation
    of the southern peasants.

41

Study Outline	Notes and Sources

f. The folk characteristics of
    southern Italian Catholicism fit
    perfectly with its social environ-
    ment. But when the attempt was
    made to transplant it to America,
    inevitable conflict arose with the
    urbanized, nationalistic, law, and
    organization oriented Irish Cathol-
    icism. The latter interpreted its
    Italian counterpart as a survival
    of pre-Christian and medieval be-
    lief and practices.

Femminella, "The Impact of Italian Migration and American Catholicism."

g. American Catholicism was unable to
    maintain even the little adherence
    to the formal Church which Italians
    possessed before coming to the U.S.
    Italians rejected the American
    Church because it exclusively spoke
    English. It was too Jansenistic.
    It stressed too heavily reverence
    and loyalty to the clergy. It was
    socially too activistic. It was
    politically too conservative. It
    was too interested in fund raising.
    And it was too identified with the
    Irish.

Sartorio, Social and Religious Life.

Mangano, Sons of Italy.

h. The Irish clergy and hierarchy who
    dominated the American Church

Linkh, American Catholicism.

42

unfortunately failed to understand
and accept the Italian peasant and
his form of Catholicism. Italian
American Catholics were soon dis-
criminated against by American
Catholicism for being vulgar, backward, irreligious, and heathens.

C. As a greater and greater number of   Felici, Father to the Immigrants.
Italians migrated to America, some
Church leaders in Italy began efforts
to help these immigrant faithful.

1. The great apostle of Italian immigrants Bishop Giovanni Battista
Scalabrini of Piacenze in 1887
founded the Apostolic College of
Priests to train clergy strictly
for pastoral work among the Italians
overseas.

2. In 1890, a Scalabrinian priest,   Francesconi, Immigrants and Priests.
Pietro Bandini, founded the San
Raffaello Society which provided
material as well as spiritual assistance to arriving Italian immigrants.

3. Nuns also came to the immigrants'   Maynard, Too Small a World; Owens,
aid. Francesca Xavier Cabrini in   "Frances Xavier Cabrini."
1889 decided to devote her entire
life to the needs of Italian

Americans. Under her leadership,

the Missionary Sisters of the Sacred

Heart established hospitals, schools,

and orphanages for Italians in the

U.S. Other Orders such as the Reli-

gious Teachers Filippini, the

Pallotine Sisters, and the Missionary

Zelatrices of the Sacred Heart also

contributed invaluable efforts for

the general welfare of the Italian

immigrants.

D. But these too few devoted nuns and   Mangano, Sons of Italy ; Shriver, Story
    priests who sacrificed their lives for   of Presbyterian Work.
    the physical and spiritual welfare of

    Italian Americans were unable to fill

    the large void left in the Italians'

    religious training and devotion by the

    intransigent refusal of the American

    Irish Catholic Church to understand

    and accept the peculiar Italian forms

    of Catholicism.

1. The Protestant Churches, especially   Mondello, "Protestant Proselytism Among
    the Evangelicals, found in this void   Italians"; Rose, Italians in America.
    much fertile ground for conversions.

    Their chief method of proselytizing

    among Italian Americans was to com-

    bine such necessities as language

    skills, financial, and material aid

with religious instruction. This
approach converted to Protestantism
a larger number of Italians than
the Catholic Church or its apologists
care to admit.

2. Part of the void was also filled by
   the radical, anarchical, and socialist elements among the Italian
   American immigrants. These in-   Vecoli, "Prelates and Peasants."
   dividuals attempted to rechannel the
   Italians' religious fervor and un-
   certainties into political ideolo-
   gies. But too few of the illiterate
   southern Italian peasants either understood or cared to be involved in
   such political activism.

3. The majority of Italian Americans   Browne, "The Italian Problem."
   simply fell away from the Church
   completely. How to bring them back
   and somehow integrate them into the
   existing institution, thereby Ameri-
   canizing them, became American
   Catholicism's "Italian Problem."

E. Italian Americans, however, were not   Barry, Catholic Church and German
   alone in their displeasure with the   Americans.
   Irish American Catholic Church. In
   1891, the German Americans, through
   what became known as the "Cahensly

Movement," expressed open dissatisfaction with the Irish dominated
Church. They requested their own ethnic parishes with German priests, customs, beliefs, rituals, feasts, and
language. Although at first resisted
as a possible schism, the "Cahensly
Movement" was ultimately understood to
be a legitimate request by a segment
of the Catholic faithful. The Holy
See finally seized upon the Germans'
request as a possible solution to the
Church's problems with immigrants.

F. But the Irish dominated American
    Catholic Church was reluctant to allow
    these foreigners separate facilities
    for fear they might prolong their
    foreignness.

    1. The Church was already under attack
        in America for its foreign origins
        and its foreign seat of power.

    2. To ward off such accusations of
        being unpatriotic and un-American,
        the U.S. Catholic Church had decided
        not only to bring the immigrant new-
        comers into her existing institu-
        tions, but also to use her organiza-
        tional structure and processes to

assimilate and ultimately Americanize
these new non-English speaking for-
eigners.

3. Only after a long series of trials,   Tomasi , Piety and Power.
    errors, and disastrous failures was   (Tomasi's is the newest and best
    the American Catholic Church able to   scholarship on the Italian Americans
    solve this tension between keeping   and the Catholic Church.)
    the immigrants faithful and Ameri-
    canizing them.

    a. The Church initially attempted to
        integrate the Italians into her
        Irish congregations. However, she
        treated them as fallen Catholics
        or pagans who must be instructed
        in the proper faith.

    b. When this failed, the Church per-
        mitted the Italians to worship in
        their own manner, but again within
        existing congregations. This sys-
        tem found the Italians relegated
        to the basements of the churches,
        preached at in broken Italian or
        vulgar Latin by an Irish American
        priest.

    c. Finally, after additional failures,
        rebellions, and losses of faithful,
        the American Catholic Church re-
        lented and allowed Italians to

build their own "National Parishes"
where Italian priests officiated
at Italian rituals during Italian
holydays in the Italian tongue.

G. But the establishment of "National   Tomasi, "The Ethnic Church."
Parishes" did not immediately solve
the "Italian Problem." For the Ital-   Femminella, "The Impact of Italian
ian Americans now reverted back to   Migration."
their own specific brand of Catholi-
cism which held formal religion in
very low esteem.

1. A serious problem emerged with the   Vecoli, "Prelates and Peasants."
Italian clergy which first arrived
in America to officiate in these new
ethnic parishes. Many had been exiled from Italian churches due to
their irreligious behavior. The
persistence of their immoral con-
duct in America only reinforced the
Italians' general dislike of the
clergy.

2. Italians frequently refused to support their new parishes. In Italy
the Church was state-supported.
Italian Americans at first found it
difficult "to pay in order to pray."

3. The Italian American still remained
a "horizontal Catholic," using the

Church only for baptism, marriage,
and his funeral. The only other in-
stance when Italians would turn out
in large numbers at their respective
Churches was to celebrate the feasts
(festa) of the saints which protected
their native Italian villages. And
these celebrations were as much a
bachanal as they were religious in
nature.

4. When these "National Parishes" made
   attempts to educate the Italian
   Americans, they also met strong re-
   sistance from the Italians' distrust
   of formal education.

H. This brief history still does not an-   McBride, "Italian Americans and the
   swer the question originally asked of   Catholic Church."
   whether or not the Catholic Church was
   ever successful in its efforts to
   assimilate and to Americanize the
   Italian immigrants.

1. Some scholars believe it did, for   (This is principally Tomasi's contention.)
   the Church was able to fill the void
   left by the disintegration in America
   of the Italian family. It also
   helped maintain ethnic solidarity.
   And it prepared the immigrants for
   American life and society. Especially

with the "National Parishes" the
Church was able to become a bridge
which the immigrants might cross
from their native culture to American society.

2. Some scholars argue the Church was   (This view is held by Vecoli.)
    no help at all to the immigrants.
    They insist the immigrants in Ameri-
    ca persisted in their hatred of the
    clergy and of formal religion. They
    discover inordinate numbers of im-
    migrants joining socialist and an-
    archist organizations. But these
    scholars are perhaps placing too
    much emphasis on the rhetoric of
    the "Italian Problem" and not enough
    emphasis on the realities of Church
    attendance and involvement especially
    after the emergence of the "National
    Parish." One must accept the in-
    fluence exerted by the Church to
    unite the Italians to form an ethnic
    entity which in time fought for
    power, influence, and its proper
    share of the American dream.

3. Perhaps, it is time to find a middle   (This is Meloni's view which will be fur-
    ground, a more accurate interpreta-   ther explained in a forthcoming article.)
    tion, between these two extreme

positions.

a. The American Irish Catholic Church
    in and of itself, was obviously a
    failure in its attempts to assimi-
    late and to Americanize.

b. But the National Parish, still
    dominated by the Irish hierarchy,
    did not completely fail at the
    same tasks. Yet, it retarded assi-
    milation and thus worked against
    the Catholic Church's hope that it
    would prove the solution and the
    fulfillment of its Americanizing
    efforts.

c. The "National Parish" kept the   Diggins, "American Catholics and Italian
    Italian American an Italian for a   Fascism."
    longer period of time than he
    otherwise might have remained.
    It recreated and maintained for
    him through its religious cele-
    brations and social activities
    his national heritage.

d. But the "National Church" did ful-
    fill an important function. It
    contributed to the creation of a
    unified Italian American ethnic
    group.

e. And it was this unity fostered by

the "National Parish" which enabled
the Italians to assert their proper
rights within the American nation.
Once America recognized their legitimate demands, Italians were on
their way to assimilation and
Americanization. Ironically, this
successful process also marked the
death knell of the "National
Parish."

I.   Today, Italian American Catholics are   Russo, "Three Generations of Italians."
mainly of the third and fourth genera-
tion.

1.   With the changes in attitudes and   Abramson, Ethnic Diversity.
prosperity after W.W. II, many Ital-   (Much of what appears in this section is
ian Americans began to send their   based on acceptance of Abramson's asser-
children to Catholic schools.   tions.)

2.   At these institutions the Italian
Americans met fellow non-Italian
Catholics. Numerous intermarriages
resulted especially with the Irish.

3.   And today these Italian Americans
are returning to the Church with
greater fervor. But the new Catholic
Church which is emerging appears to
be a replica in beliefs and structure of the old Irish American Catholicism.

Study Outline	*Notes and Sources*

4. Thus, the Catholic Church does appear to have helped, with qualifications, the Italian American toward Americanization. It successfully began the process but could not complete it. The Church retarded assimilation rather than promote it through the "National Parishes." But they too indirectly helped in the ultimate triumph. Yet, it was education, intermarriage, and the passing of time and generations which finally achieved the Americanization of Italian Americans. Oddly enough, the final result has still been to "Hibernize" the Italian Americans--precisely the self assigned mission of the original Irish American Church.

(This is a strictly personal summation.)

III. Conclusion

For at least the first generation of Italian Americans, the Catholic Church proved to be of only limited social and cultural assistance. The Church was too occupied with its own ethnic and political controversies to be of any serious consequence to the original Italians who arrived in ever increasing numbers between 1870 and 1920.

Having slowly lost their traditional family structure and finding little aid from institutionalized religion, the Italian American turned to other types of associational and organizational life. He sought from mutual benefit societies, from the immigrant press, from politics, and from crime alternative institutional means to achieve economic affluence, social stability, political advantage, and personal gratification.

CHAPTER FIVE: IMMIGRANT ORGANIZATIONAL ALTERNATIVES

I. Introduction

The American people found it difficult to agree how the nation's newcomers should be absorbed into the mainstream of American life. The proponents of the "melting-pot" theory saw eventual homogeneity emerging from the various ethnic groups. But some Americans felt the nation should not even wait for this eventuality, but rather make an all out effort to Americanize the immigrants as quickly as possible. Toward this goal, America should severely limit the number of new immigrants as well as their quality. Only those peoples most amenable to the White Anglo-Saxon Protestant ideal should be allowed to enter the U.S. But, the advocates of pluralism countered with their theory of an America growing stronger and richer through a vast mixture of diverse and unregenerated ethnic differences.

Before immigration restriction became a reality in 1924, the Italians had been unable to seek their proper niche within American society due to the vast numbers of their countrymen who daily arrived to the U.S. These arrivals had enabled Italian Americans to keep alive the old customs, ideas, and language within the various "Little Italys." But between 1924 and W.W. II, Italian Americans, no longer excessively reminded of their homeland by new arrivals, began to make accommodations with their host society. And as their old Italian organizational structures, such as the family, began to disintegrate, they turned to new institutions such as the mutual benefit societies, politics, the press, and crime.

After an early period of fanatical admiration for Benito Mussolini, one of the factors which united Italian Americans of diverse regions, dialects, and villages into one ethnic entity, the Italians in America found it expedient to endorse the American war effort against Italy. This became even more pressing as the true menace of Fascism became more evident. With this endorsement, most Italian Americans realized that perhaps after W.W. II, it would be more accurate to speak of themselves as American Italians rather than vice versa.

II. Guide and Sourcebook

Study Outline	*Notes and Sources*
A. Many Italian American immigrants solved their alienation, loneliness, despair, and all other adverse consequences of their new lives by joining what became known as "mutual benefit societies."	Nelli, Italians in Chicago. (Nelli is one of the few historians who has studied this organizational and institutional phenomena among immigrants in any kind of detail.)
1. These institutions were not transplanted by southern Italians to the	Banfield, The Moral Basis.

Study Outline	*Notes and Sources*

U.S., for in southern Italy, where
family relationships assured assistance in time of need, group life
was limited to recreational activities in social clubs (circolo
sociale). These groups had small
memberships and no community importance.

(Much of this section, however, depends
heavily on Nelli's explorations of the
subject.)

2. The mutual benefit society (società
di mutuo soccorso) did exist in
Italy, but only among the middle
class artisans in the urbanized
sections of northern and central
Italy.

Clark, Our Italian Fellow Citizen.

(They most certainly did not exist in any
of the regions which contributed the
heaviest "new immigration" to America.)

3. But there were important differences
between these Italian mutual benefit
societies and those established in
America. In Italy, these groups
were closely allied with the growth
of labor unions. In the U.S., they
concentrated on insurance and social
functions, aiding new immigrants in
dealing with sickness, loneliness,
and death rather than with labor.

Nelli, Italians in Chicago.

Rodgers, "Migration and Industrial Development."

4. Immigrants who joined these societies contributed small monthly sums
to guarantee that the group would
look after them when sick, and

Iorizzo and Mondello, Italian Americans.

provide a decent burial when dead.
All members were to attend funerals
or pay a fine. This was how the
organization assured each member a
proper and well-attended burial.
Consequently, funerals became social
events where old acquaintances
gathered to reminisce about the old
days in the old country.

5. These mutual aid groups were purely
    voluntary and cooperative enter-
    prises. Unfortunately, they often
    operated on unsound actuarial prin-
    ciples.

    (Numerous sharp operators used these
    groups to their own personal advantage
    rather than for the benefit of the mem-
    bers.)

6. The groups were small and mostly
    organized according to respective
    Italian villages or dialects. But
    their profusion and inadequate funds
    drove them toward consolidation.
    Ignorance of sound insurance prac-
    tices also played its part in this
    process. And the societies were
    ultimately absorbed into fraternal
    organizations.

    Biagi, The Purple Aster.

7. It was primarily financial consider-
    ations which speeded the process for
    consolidation of these small mutual
    benefit societies into larger

    De Conde, Half Bitter, Half Sweet.

Study Outline	*Notes and Sources*

fraternal insurance groups organized
along regional and later along
national lines. Groups like the
Italo-American National Union and
the Sons of Italy emerged as a consequence of their sound insurance
practices.

8. But in order to attract and hold
   membership, these fraternals ex-
   panded their services from the basic
   benefit function to include social
   activities. Among these were the
   provisions for recreational facili-
   ties and special annual events such
   as picnics, dances, and religious
   celebrations.

Heiss, "Satisfaction and Assimilation."

9. Besides the mutual benefit societies
   and the fraternals, there were other
   groups which originated from and for
   military, political, religious, or
   anti-religious objectives. But too
   many of these organizations, along
   with some of the mutual benefit and
   fraternal groups, began to spend too
   much time, money, and efforts on
   monument building, patriotic celebrations, and other manifestations
   of loyalty either to Italy or to

Lopreato, Italian Americans.

Tomasi, Piety and Power.
(Tomasi gives a detailed discussion of
these individuals, as does Nelli in his
Italians in Chicago.)

(Unfortunately, still today too many
Italian Americans are expanding much

America. They began to spend more
than the immigrants could afford.
And their actual material results
for the betterment of the Italian
Americans' life were too few to
justify their expenses.

time, effort, and money on medals, monuments, and fundraising.)

10. But all of these various societies
also served a good purpose. They
helped to develop a feeling of identity within the various Italian
American colonies. This encouraged
Italians from all regions, villages,
and dialects to see themselves as
one identifiable national ethnic
group. Through such a recognition
Italian Americans were able to exert
political, social, cultural, and
economic influence upon the larger
American society.

De Conde, Half Bitter, Half Sweet.
(De Conde depicts this evolution toward
ethnic identity quite well.)

B. The Italian-language press in America
afforded Italian Americans another
link through which they might unite
and organize. It also provided news
of the mother country which during
the early years of migration helped
Italian Americans combat their loneliness and despair.

Study of the Italian Language Press.

Cordasco, Italian Community and Its
Language.

1. Except for the few socialist and

Diggins, Mussolini and Fascism; "Mussolini

Study Outline	*Notes and Sources*

anarchist newspapers , most of the Italian American press was loyal to its host nation. After the brief romance with Mussolini's nationalism, much of the Italian-language press in America supported the American war effort.

and America"; "Italo-American Anti-Fascist."

2. The large number of Italian American newspapers which originally flourished in the U.S. ultimately failed due to the restriction on the constant new waves of Italian immigrants coming to America. Furthermore, Italian Americans became the most notorious of the immigrant groups which soon after arriving in America lacked native language maintenance efforts. Within two generations most Italian Americans could barely speak a few words of the old family dialect, much less any extensive amounts of the pure mother tongue.

(A lecture by Joshua Fishman recorded in Cordasco's Italian Community explains in depth the language maintenance problems of the Italian community.)

3. Thus, at their worst Italian-language newspapers kept the immigrants tied to the past, and they retarded their assimilative process. But at their best, they also helped the immigrants to see themselves as

Nelli, Italians in Chicago.

Italian Americans with definite rights and obligations resulting from the latter portion of their identity.

C. Most of the immigrant newcomers to America have sooner or later recognized that one of the avenues to the fulfillment of the American dream is politics. And the Italian Americans were no exception in this recognition.

Barbaro, "Ethnic Affirmation."

1. The Irish Americans early emerged as natural political leaders. They knew representative government, the mechanics of elections, the role of the press, the importance of organization, and above all, they spoke the language.

Iorizzo and Mondello, Italian Americans.

2. But for the "new immigrants" it was a more difficult story. Coming from eastern, central, and southern Europe they were strangers to the processes of democracy. This was compounded by their exclusion from society's better jobs, their general illiteracy, and their ignorance of English.

Douglas, Influence of South Italians; Banfield, Moral Basis.

3. The Italians were the largest ethnic group of this "new immigration."

La Gumina, Wop; De Conde, Half Bitter, Half Sweet.

They were viewed as inferior to the American Anglo-Saxon stocks. They were a threat to the American northern European peoples who were believed to be more free, energetic, progressive, and democratic. The southern European was assessed as a downtrodden, atavistic, and stagnant individual. In politics, Americans feared these "new immigrants" might surrender power to the demogagic "machine bosses."

4. These "new immigrants," Americans believed, would inevitably become the tools of political corruption since they were incapable of democratic assimilation due to their lack of an Anglo-Saxon heritage. The Italians especially might fall victims to the evils of "ward bossism."

(La Gumina once again through actual historical documents proves this discrimination most poignantly.)

5. The "ward bosses" extracted payment in the form of votes from the Italians for the opportunity to befriend and aid them. Some scholars have compared these "ward bosses" to social workers except that they demanded a feudal-lord vassal relation-

Ernst, _Immigrant Life_; Rolle, _American Italians_; Nelli, _Italians in Chicago_. (One should not easily forget that too often these devoted social workers were most anxious to Americanize and assimilate the immigrant at all costs. Their intentions may have been good ones, but their

ship with the potential voters. The
chief difference was that the social
settlement workers were not so demanding or corruptive. Yet, it is
debatable whether the social workers
themselves did not extract from the
immigrants their own social, even if
not political, concessions in order
to lead them to assimilation and
Americanization.

results were often disastrous with regard
to the immigrants' ethnic identity.)

6. The initial political leaders within
the "Little Italys" were those Italian Americans who had settled in
America permanently, learned the
language, made some economic ad-
vances, and could serve as inter-
mediaries with both the Italian
and American governments.

Tomasi, Piety and Power.
(Tomasi draws a very fine historical
sketch of these "Prominenti.")

   a. But these individuals (prominenti)
did very little to unite the Italians into an effective political
force. Indeed, they often legiti-
mized their position by identi-
fying themselves as the apostles
of Italianness (Italianità).

   b. Through their contacts with the
Italian government, these "prominenti" organized the efforts and

Ware, Greenwich Village.
(Needless to say, there are still individuals making a living pushing

Study Outline	Notes and Sources

the funds of Italian Americans to award medals of recognition, to build monuments, to raise money for Italian catastrophies, and to celebrate Italian holidays. The Italian government gladly played along with this myth of "Italianità." But, all these efforts and dollars, though laudable, gained for Italians no political, social, or economic concessions from the larger American community.

7. To break into the American political structure, Italians had to begin at the local level and displace other already entrenched ethnic groups such as the Irish and the Germans.

8. The older groups in power came to appreciate the importance of a "solid" Italian vote. To achieve this end, they allowed a select few Italians to enter the ruling clique of the "ward bosses." And after these initial victories, the Italian Americans, as they came to realize that changes in the laws was the best means to improve their lives, proceeded to grasp for larger shares of

Italianità. But instead of politics and economics, their chief occupation today is academia. They are the members of the "spaghetti and tarantella" school of Italian American history. They are little more than "filiopietists." While still performing a service to their ethnic community, they do present certain problems detailed in a later chapter.)

Nelli, Italians in Chicago.

(It is Nelli again who has carried out the most extensive research in the area of Italian American political origins and early successes.)

Study Outline	*Notes and Sources*
the political prizes and rewards.	

9. After W.W. I, the Republican Party recruited Italians to counter the strength of the Irish Democratic machines. And many Italian Americans joined happily because of the historical association the name of that Party had with Garibaldi. But most switched to the Democrats once Franklin D. Roosevelt appeared on the national scene. Yet, when he opposed the Ethiopian War and favored sanctions against Italy, many Italian Americans returned to the ranks of the G.O.P.

Tortosa, "Italian Americans."

De Conde, *Half Bitter, Half Sweet.*

Diggins, *Mussolini and Fascism.*

10. It was not long before Italian Americans had prominent political leaders on the national scene. Men such as Fiorello H. La Guardia, elected to Congress from 1916 to 1932, and Vito Marcantonio, elected from 1934 to 1950, became symbols of Italian American political skill, leadership, and accomplishment.

Garrett, *La Guardia.*

Zinn, *La Guardia.*

11. Many of these Italian American politicians have been accused of being "machine bosses." They are depicted as socialists or communists. They

Iorizzo and Mondello, *Italian Americans.*

are condemned for their alleged at-
tachments to criminality. But, it
should be remembered that these men
were for the most part "progressives"
and social visionaries far ahead of
their time or colleagues. They always provided their electorate with
what it needed--a means of coping
with hostility from most of society.
They enabled the poor immigrants to
maintain a semblance of decency and
self-respect. Their constituency,
often on the verge of poverty and
despair, was impressed with their
concrete assistance rather than
with vague political philosophies
and visions. And many of their
programs, having lost their socialist and communist tinge, are today
most effective and productive in
the larger American society.

12. Today, Italian Americans have moved
    into all aspects and levels of local
    and national politics. But they
    have emerged as a middle class con-
    servative force. Because he is
    still uncertain about his acceptance
    or image within American society,

Cordasco, Studies in Social History.

Novak, Unmeltable Ethnics.

the Italian has become more American than the Americans, more nationalist than the Daughters of the American Revolution. He is a conservative nationalist belonging to the conservative wing of the Democratic Party. But he is especially numerous among the conservative Republicans. Since conservatives have in recent times been out of political power, Italian Americans have not fully surfaced to political leadership in relation to their numbers. However, should the political fortunes of liberals ever be fully reversed, Italian Americans will have more than their proper share of the American political dream.	Krickus, Pursuing the Dream. (Many of these notions are also personal conclusions based on observation and oral history.)

D. Americans have reacted to crime among Italians with frenzied emotions like no other immigrant group has aroused. Government reports, books, pamphlets, magazines, newspapers, television, films, all have analyzed and decried Italian American criminality.

Nelli, "Italians in Crime."
(As in so many other areas, Nelli is the only contemporary historian of Italian American history who has delved deeply and in a scholarly fashion into Italian American criminality.)

1. But before January 16, 1920 most Italian crimes took place only within "Little Italys," and they

Whyte, Street Corner Society.

affected only its resi-ents.

2. Yet, the turning point for America's view of Italian criminality came with the New Orleans Affair of 1890. David Hennessy, the New Orleans chief of police, was mortally shot on October 15, 1890. Before dying, he was heard to say, "The dagos shot me." On November 9, the Grand Jury indicted 19 Italians. Only 9 were placed on trial, and found not guilty. But 20,000 outraged New Orleans citizens on March 14, 1891 marched to the prison where the Italians were still jailed in spite of acquittal. They shot and clubbed the prisoners to death. As a result of this outrage, the Italian and American governments nearly went to war.

Coxe, "New Orleans"; Karlin, "New Orleans Lynchings"; "Italo-American Incident"; Kendall, "Who Killa de Chief?"

3. After this New Orleans Affair, Italian Americans found themselves branded as a dangerous and criminal class. It was suggested that a vast Italian criminal organization called "Mafia" permeated all of American society.

Albini, The American Mafia.

4. In order to show that criminality among Italians was not a transplanted

Nelli, Italians in Chicago.

institution, but only isolated instances of localized crimes by a few
Italian American criminals, the
Italian immigrant press began re-
ferring to all crimes within "Little
Italys" as Black Hand offenses. The
label stuck.

5. Soon Italians throughout America were
forming White Hand Societies to
counter the evils of these few way-
ward immigrants in their midst.

6. But the original Mafia had its origins in the Sicilian Vespers of the
Thirteen Century when Sicilians attempted to rid the Island of the
French. Indeed, it may even date
back to when Sicilian slaves re-
volted against the Romans. These
secret societies became the means
whereby Sicilians could achieve justice against foreign invaders. In
time this Mafia served as a means
for Sicilians to get justice from
other Sicilians. And the institution always escaped eradication, no
matter how great or valiant the effort, due to its sacred code of si-
lence (omertà).

Blok, *Mafia of a Sicilian Village*;
Iorizzo and Mondello, "Origins of Italian
Criminality."

7. The Mafia did come to America with the immigrants. But it could be a benevolent as well as an evil force. Within the "Little Italys" the local Mafiosi assured the immigrants justice against their fellow immigrants and against the American society.

Sassone, "Italy's Criminality."

a. Obviously, the opportunities for these Mafiosi to pursue evil as well as good became apparent and easily available. The Mafioso might exploit immigrant laborers. He might shake down small Italian businessmen. But, he might also offer both protection. He could act as a strong paternalistic presence in the immigrant community. He often took the roles of judge, lawgiver, defender of tradition, and moralist.

Nelli, "Italians in Crime."

b. Other southern Italians also transplanted criminal institutions to America. The Calabrians had the "Fibbia," while the Neapolitans had the "Camorra." Both, however, were strictly criminal organizations. And neither achieved much sustained success in America.

Nelli, Business of Crime.

Study Outline	*Notes and Sources*

8. The first distinctively Italian criminality to emerge from the "Little Italys" came from Black Hand (Mano Nera) criminals. These might or might not also belong to some local Mafia group.

Sondern, Brotherhood.

   a. These Black Hand criminals practiced a form of banditry which has existed for centuries in poverty ridden societies throughout the world.

Schiavo, The Truth About the Mafia.

   b. They preyed off Italian Americans who had managed to gain some means of affluence. They practiced extortion, terrorism, labor agent abuses, illegal banking schemes, and juvenile delinquency.

Landesco, Organized Crime.

   c. These neighborhood gangs filled an important social void. They did introduce the young Italian Americans to a life of crime. But, they also offered a quick and substantial monetary gain and success within an American society which valued such ends above the means employed to achieve them.

Whyte, Street Corner Society.

9. But before 1920, most arrests of Italian Americans were for

Mariano, Immigrants' Day in Court.

misdemeanors and violations of city
ordinances of which most Italians
were not cognizant.

10. Then Prohibition opened a new crimi-
    nal occupation which had less risk
    of punishment, more certainty of
    gain, and less social stigma.

Nelli, Business of Crime.

   a. When Italians arrived to America,
    they found economic advancement
    difficult due to inadequate educa-
    tion, their social background,
    and a lack o political connec-
    tions. But Prohibition in 1920
    offered a new field of economic
    endeavor, one in which the only
    required qualifications were am-
    bition, ruthlessness, and loyalty.

Schiavo, The Truth About the Mafia.

   b. Nationally organized groups of
    criminals were present and oper-
    ating in America long before the
    Italians arrived. They possessed
    both police and political protec-
    tion. And with the coming of
    Prohibition, Italians joined these
    societies. They slowly climbed
    their organizational ladders. And
    after reaching the top, they have
    since remained in control in spite

Hess, Mafia and Mafiosi.

of recent challenges from the
emerging Black and Puerto Rican
powers.

c. Italians achieved great successes   Nelli, The Business of Crime.
    in organized crime because through
    Prohibition, they came to look
    upon criminality as simply a new
    form of business enterprise. From
    bootlegging, they applied these
    same principles to loan sharking,
    gambling, prostitution, strike-
    breaking, and murder. And the new
    organizational frameworks they de-
    vised to promote their business be-
    came the "Mafia" syndicates.

d. The old timers had wanted to keep   Martin, Revolt in the Mafia.
    the "Mafia" as it had been in
    Sicily and in its early American
    days. But, by 1930 these "Mustache
    Petes," as they were jokingly re-
    ferred to, were brutally eliminated
    by the younger members during the
    "Night of the Sicilian Vespers."

e. Young leaders like Al Capone saw   Kobler, The Life of Al Capone.
    themselves as businessmen pro-
    viding a product to customers who
    came from all of society. And
    they flourished during a period of

unrestrained materialist American culture.

f. But by the 1940s these younger members had also grown old, been jailed, or died. They were replaced by a more cohesive, back to family-centered structure which Joseph Valachi in 1964 called "Our Thing" (La Cosa Nostra).

Mass, <u>Valachi Papers</u>.

11. The Black Hand and the Mafia had earlier existed principally as a means of survival, but never as formal organizations. But once Italian Americans seized power within organized crime, then the Mafia became an institutionalized reality.

12. And because crime has been for some Italian Americans of the Third and Fourth generations a means of economic betterment and social upward mobility, it must occupy the Italian Americans' assimilation into the mainstream of American society. Whether for it or against it, crime has united Italian Americans. It has made them forget their "old world" differences. Italian Americans should place their heritage of

Bell, "Crime As a Way of Life."

Nelli, <u>Business of Crime</u>.

criminality in its proper historical

perspective. They should stop being

so edgy about its existence or truth.

And though not proud of it, they

should recognize that it has been

for some, directly or indirectly,

a passport to a fuller share of the

American political, social, and eco-

nomic dream.

13. But today, official government pres-

sures, the advancing age of syndi-

cate leaders, and the inability to

attract young talent, combined with

the stiff competition from Blacks

and Latins are marking the beginning

of the end for Italian American Mafia

control of America's organized crimi-

nal syndicates.

III. Conclusion

Irregardless of the institutional means employed by Italians to survive and to
succeed in American society, it is the opinion of many scholars that Italian Americans
have indeed arrived in our lifetime to at least a partial fulfillment of the American
dream. For these historians, sociologists, and social critics, it is no longer valid
to speak of Italian Americans. They insist that this ethnic group can only correctly
be referred to as American Italians.

CHAPTER SIX: THE AMERICAN ITALIANS

I. Introduction

Despite their numbers, it is only in recent times that Italian Americans in the United States have begun to achieve a status of genuine respect at all levels of society. For the most part, Italian Americans are still lagging behind other major ethnic groups from Europe in wealth, status, and influence. Part of the explanation for this situation is the nature and the timing of the Italian American immigration process. Italians were the last and most depressed of the immigrants who arrived in large numbers before restriction. They have had farther to reach and in less time than most other ethnic groups.

Italian Americans have survived in spite of the bitterness of their experiences, their sufferings, and the discrimination. Scholars have decried the cruelty of the Italian American immigrant process and experience. But, Italians and their descendants appear finally today to have found their rightful place within American society. Or have they? It is true that some have completely Americanized and are indistinguishable from the predominant Anglo-Saxon Protestant ethnics. But many Italian Americans, especially those of the third and fourth generations, are still searching, perhaps not so much in economic terms, but surely in their culture and assuredly in their spirits, for the true explanations and meanings of their existence in contemporary America. And their perplexities are often caused by the confused status of their ethnic heritage.

II. Guide and Sourcebook

Study Outline	*Notes and Sources*
A. Some scholars maintain that ethnic groups in America tend to pass through three distinct stages.	Gambino, Blood of My Blood. (Much of the conceptualization in this first section comes from Gambino's personal reflections.)
1. The first stage is that time when the ethnic group lacks the access to the larger host society. This is characteristic only of the purely immigrant first generation period of immigration.	
2. The second stage takes place when the ethnic group's second generation blames itself for, feels guilty of, and is ashamed in its differences	

from the host society's dominant

ethnicity. As a result, this genera-

tion subordinates itself to the

majority group.

3. The third stage offers two alterna-

tives to the later generations.

a. The ethnic group can allow the old

values and traditions to disappear

totally and perfectly assimilate.

b. Or it can revitalize the old   (The terms are Gambino's, the interpre-

values and customs of the original   tation and definitions are personal.)

immigrant generation. This it

can do in several ways and forms.

1) It can revitalize itself into

a "transparent non-identity.

Through this, it only play acts

at its old ethnicity , thereby

not using it for any social,

political, economic , or cul-

tural advantage.

2) It can revitalize itself with

"charismatic ethnocentrism."

This means emphasizing the tri-

balistic ethnic customs for the

purpose of boasting the group's

worth. It is also called

"filiopietism." And it is often

employed to gain concessions

from the majority group in order
to achieve ultimate unity with,
rather than distinction from it.

3) Or the group can revitalize itself through "creative ethnicity." This is a genuine ap-
preciation for and adherence to
the group's original values and
traditions modified for the ex-
ixting times and circumstances.
The group employs its ethnic
heritage to achieve its rightful
position within society, while
in the process it appreciates
and learns to respect the ethnic
foundations of all other groups,
be they more powerful or dis-
possessed.

B. In the U.S. in 1970, there were more
Italians than in any other country in
the world except for Italy itself.

1. Unfortunately, Italian Americans today view themselves as failures.
They see everything about them as
being inferior, cheap, ridiculous,
or criminal. American society has
encouraged them to feel this way
through its contemporary slang,

De Conde, Half Bitter, Half Sweet.
(De Conde does an admirable job in his
last few chapters of generalizing and
conceptualizing the entirety of the
Italian American experience. And the
introduction to this chapter owes much
to De Conde's work.)

attitudes, and media-culture. And
Italians seem to respond favorably
and willingly to this.

2. Italian Americans appear to forget
that except for the exploited masses
of the great industrial cities of
Europe in the Nineteenth Century,
Italian peasants in the U.S. led
more burdensome and more degrading
lives than did other comparable
classes of American or European
workers.

C. Today the Italian American finds himself in the third stage of the immigration process. And he does appear
at times to be choosing to revitalize
his old ethnic values and customs.
Yet, the Italians must now decide if
their ethnicity will be transparent
non-identity, charismatic, or creative.

1. This decision the Italian Americans
can only make by and for themselves.
But in the process they need more
ethnic affirmation, more collective
action, less involvement in the sub-
cultures, and more commitment to the
socio-political life of the larger
ethnic society. And most important,

Barbaro, "Ethnic Affirmation."
(Many of the ideas expressed in this
last section have been suggested by the
Barbaro article.)

they must not lose sight of their
ultimate ethnic objectives.

2. To achieve any meaningful revitali-
zation of their ethnicity, Italian
Americans also need several other
factors to be present.

   a. They need a hospitable environ-
ment. And American society does
today appear, on the surface at
least, to be most favorably dis-
posed toward the renewed emphases
and celebrations of ethnicity and
roots.

   b. They need strong dissatisfactions
with their present circumstances.
And today Italian Americans,
finding themselves lumped together
with all other white ethnics, are
becoming increasingly upset over
the discriminations and prejudices
exercised against them through
hiring and promotion practices,
which follow Federal guidelines
of Equal Opportunity.

   c. Finally, they need a strong leadership. Yet, this is precisely
the third and vital ingredient for
renewed ethnicity which Italian

(Today there are more and more Italian
Americans expressing their ethnic con-
sciousness through literature and poetry.
Though not dealt with directly in this
brief survey, the work of these artists
is capably analyzed in Green, _Italian
American Novel_ and in the last chapters of
De Conde, _Half Bitter, Half Sweet_.)

Americans seem to be lacking in

greatest quantities at present.

III. Conclusion

The future directions and accomplishments of this renewed ethnic vitality of Italian Americans remain in doubt. But in spite of the outcome, no one can any longer deny that Italian American history is the saga of a remarkable and diverse people with a rich and varied background, who fashioned through suffering, deprivation, and hard work a living memorial to man's inability to prevent his fellows from their rightful claim upon the earth's bounties.

APPENDIX

ITALIAN IMMIGRATION TO THE UNITED STATES BY YEARS

Year	Number	Year	Number	Year	Number	Year	Number	Year	Number	Year	Number
1820	30	1845	137	1870	2,891	1895	35,427	1920	95,145	1945	213
1821	63	1846	151	1871	2,816	1896	68,060	1921	222,260	1946	2,636
1822	35	1847	164	1872	4,190	1897	59,431	1922	40,319	1947	13,866
1823	33	1848	241	1873	8,757	1898	58,613	1923	46,674	1948	16,075
1824	45	1849	209	1874	7,666	1899	77,419	1924	56,246	1949	11,695
1825	75	1850	431	1875	3,631	1900	100,135	1925	6,203	1950	12,454
1826	57	1851	447	1876	3,015	1901	135,996	1926	8,253	1951	8,958
1827	35	1852	351	1877	3,195	1902	178,375	1927	17,297	1952	11,342
1828	34	1853	555	1878	4,344	1903	230,622	1928	17,728	1953	8,434
1829	23	1854	1,263	1879	5,791	1904	193,296	1929	18,008	1954	13,145
1830	9	1855	1,052	1880	12,354	1905	221,479	1930	22,327	1955	30,272
1831	28	1856	1,365	1881	15,401	1906	273,120	1931	13,399	1956	40,430
1832	3	1857	1,007	1882	32,159	1907	285,731	1932	6,662	1957	19,624
1833	1,699	1858	1,240	1883	31,792	1908	128,503	1933	3,477	1958	23,115
1834	105	1859	932	1884	16,510	1909	183,218	1934	4,374	1959	16,804
1835	60	1860	1,019	1885	13,642	1910	215,537	1935	6,566	1960	13,369
1836	115	1861	811	1886	21,315	1911	182,882	1936	6,774	1961	18,956
1837	36	1862	566	1887	47,622	1912	157,134	1937	7,192	1962	20,119
1838	86	1863	547	1888	51,558	1913	265,542	1938	7,712	1963	16,175
1839	84	1864	600	1889	25,307	1914	283,738	1939	6,570	1964	12,769
1840	37	1865	924	1890	52,003	1915	49,688	1940	5,302	1965	10,874
1841	179	1866	1,382	1891	76,055	1916	33,665	1941	450	1966	26,449
1842	100	1867	1,624	1892	61,631	1917	34,596	1942	103	1967	28,487
1843	117	1868	891	1893	72,145	1918	5,250	1943	49	1968	25,882
1844	141	1869	1,489	1894	42,977	1919	1,884	1944	120	1969	27,033

Source: Luciano J. Iorizzo and Salvatore Mondello, The Italian American. P. 218.

DISTRIBUTION OF ITALIAN-BORN IMMIGRANTS BY DECADE AND STATE

	1850	1860	1870	1880	1890	1990	1910
Alabama	90	187	118	114	322	862	2,696
Arizona	--	--	T12	T104	T207	T699	1,531
Arkansas	15	17	30	132	187	576	1,699
California	228	2,805	4,660	7,537	15,495	22,777	88,504
Colorado	--	T6	T16	335	3,882	6,818	14,375
Connecticut	16	61	117	879	5,285	19,105	56,954
Delaware	--	4	5	43	459	1,122	2,893
District of Columbia	74	94	182	244	467	930	2,761
Florida	40	75	56	77	408	1,707	4,538
Georgia	33	47	50	82	159	218	545
Idaho	--	--	T11	T35	509	779	2,067
Illinois	43	219	761	1,764	8,035	23,523	72,163
Indiana	6	92	95	198	468	1,327	6,911
Iowa	1	26	54	122	399	1,198	5,846
Kansas	--	15	55	167	616	987	3,520
Kentucky	143	231	325	370	707	679	1,316
Louisiana	915	1,134	1,889	2,527	8,437	17,431	20,233
Maine	20	49	48	90	258	1,334	3,468
Maryland	82	220	210	477	1,416	2,449	6,969
Massachusetts	196	371	454	2,116	8,066	28,785	85,056
Michigan	12	78	110	555	3,088	6,178	16,861
Minnesota	T1	45	40	124	828	2,222	9,669
Mississippi	121	114	147	260	425	845	2,137
Missouri	124	554	936	1,074	2,416	4,345	12,984
Montana	--	--	T34	T64	734	2,199	6,592
Nebraska	--	T18	44	62	717	752	3,799
Nevada	--	T13	199	1,560	1,129	1,296	2,831
New Hampshire	--	18	9	32	312	947	2,071
New Jersey	30	105	277	1,547	12,989	41,865	115,446
New Mexico	T1	T11	T25	T73	T355	T661	1,959
New York	833	1,862	3,592	15,113	64,141	182,248	472,201
North Carolina	4	27	19	42	28	201	521
North Dakota	--	T1	T4	T71	21	700	1,262
Ohio	174	407	564	1,064	3,857	11,321	41,620
Oklahoma	--	--	--	--	T11	T28	2,564
Oregon	T5	33	31	167	589	1,014	5,538
Pennsylvania	172	622	784	2,794	24,682	66,655	196,122
Rhode Island	25	32	58	313	2,468	8,972	27,287
South Carolina	59	59	63	84	106	180	316
South Dakota	--	--	--	--	269	360	1,158
Tennessee	59	373	483	443	788	1,222	2,034
Texas	41	67	186	539	2,107	3,942	7,190
Utah	T1	T40	T74	T138	T347	1,062	3,117
Vermont	7	13	17	30	445	2,154	4,594
Virginia	65	259	162	281	1,219	781	2,449
Washington	--	T11	T24	T71	1,408	2,124	13,121
West Virginia	--	--	34	48	632	2,921	17,292
Wisconsin	9	103	104	253	1,123	2,172	9,273
Wyoming	--	--	T9	T15	259	781	1,961
Alaska	--					T438	
Hawaii	--					T68	
Total	3,645	10,518	17,457	44,230	182,580	484,703	1,343,125

Source: Ibid., pp. 219-220.

82

DISTRIBUTION OF ITALIAN-BORN IMMIGRANTS BY DECADE AND STATE (Concluded)

	1920	1930	1940	1950	1960
Alabama	2,732	2,140	1,699	1,436	1,151
Arizona	1,261	822	715	1,600	2,450
Arkansas	1,314	952	791	670	525
California	88,504	107,249	100,911	104,215	102,366
Colorado	12,580	10,670	8,352	6,329	4,797
Connecticut	80,322	87,123	81,373	74,270	65,233
Delaware	4,136	3,769	3,464	3,031	2,914
District of Columbia	3,764	4,330	4,913	4,422	3,086
Florida	4,745	5,262	5,138	8,087	16,217
Georgia	700	712	536	638	750
Idaho	1,323	1,153	892	633	420
Illinois	94,407	110,449	98,244	83,556	72,139
Indiana	6,712	6,873	6,309	5,508	4,756
Iowa	4,956	3,834	3,461	2,908	2,254
Kansas	3,355	2,165	1,654	1,214	1,024
Kentucky	1,932	1,589	1,302	1,067	911
Louisiana	16,264	13,526	9,849	7,678	5,470
Maine	2,797	2,359	2,268	2,008	1,568
Maryland	9,543	10,872	10,119	9,942	10,454
Massachusetts	117,007	126,103	114,362	101,458	86,921
Michigan	30,216	43,087	40,631	38,937	36,879
Minnesota	7,432	6,401	5,628	4,496	3,541
Mississippi	1,841	1,613	1,294	1,023	923
Missouri	14,609	15,242	13,168	10,695	9,033
Montana	3,842	2,840	2,265	1,767	1,055
Nebraska	3,547	3,642	3,201	2,622	1,996
Nevada	2,641	2,563	2,258	1,985	1.665
New Hampshire	2,074	1,938	1,687	1,416	1,138
New Jersey	157,285	190,858	169,063	150,680	137,356
New Mexico	1,678	1,259	1,148	934	809
New York	545,173	629,322	584,075	503,175	440,063
North Carolina	453	438	445	553	567
North Dakota	176	102	80	96	73
Ohio	60,658	71,496	65,453	56,593	50,338
Oklahoma	2,122	1,157	893	805	710
Oregon	4,324	4,728	4,083	3,581	3,024
Pennsylvania	232,764	225,979	197,281	163,359	131,149
Rhode Island	32,241	32,493	28,851	24,380	18,438
South Carolina	344	188	175	228	260
South Dakota	413	305	238	202	174
Tennessee	2,079	1,946	1,734	1,552	1,383
Texas	8,024	6,550	5,451	5,059	4,568
Utah	3,225	2,814	2,189	1,750	1,437
Vermont	4,067	2,082	2,339	1,766	1,208
Virginia	2,435	1,853	1,843	2,087	2,468
Washington	10,813	10,274	8,853	7,566	6,072
West Virginia	14,147	12,088	10,601	8,557	5,882
Wisconsin	11,188	12,599	11,086	9,663	8,479
Wyoming	1,984	1,653	1,215	858	555
Alaska					
Hawaii					
Total	1,610,113	1,790,429	1,623,580	1,427,145	1,256,999

Source: Ibid., pp. 219-220.

BIBLIOGRAPHY

This is a most "Select Bibliography." Only those books and articles which are most vital to a beginning exploration of Italian American history have been included. A further criterion for selection has been easy accessibility of the source. As a result, no unpublished dissertations, rare or obscure journal monographs, foreign language articles or books, and limited elite editions have been listed. Students, who wish to pursue the subject further, might refer to those bibliographical publications scattered throughout this limited listing.

Books

Abramson, Harold J. Ethnic Diversity in Catholic America. New York, 1973.

Albini, Joseph L. The American Mafia: Genesis of a Legend. New York, 1971.

Albrecht-Carrie, Rene. Italy from Napoleon to Mussolini. New York, 1960.

Amfitheatrof, Erik. The Children of Columbus: An Informal History of the Italians in the New World. Boston, 1973.

Asciolla, Paul J. The Contributions of Italian Americans to American Culture. New York, 1967.

A Study of the Italian Language Press in the United States. Princeton, 1942.

Baden, Anne L. Immigration in the United States: A Selected List of Recent References. Washington, D.C., 1943.

Banfield, Edward C. The Moral Basis of a Backward Society. Glencoe, 1958.

Barry, Colman J. The Catholic Church and German Americans. Milwaukee, 1953.

Beck, Frank O. The Italian in Chicago. Chicago, 1919.

Biagi, Ernest L. The Purple Aster: A History of the Order Sons of Italy in America. New York, 1961.

Bianco, Carla. The Two Rosetos. Bloomington, Indiana, 1974.

Blok, Anton. The Mafia of a Sicilian Village, 1860-1960: A Study of Violent Peasant Entrepreneurs. Oxford, 1974.

Brace, Charles Loring. The Dangerous Classes of New York and Twenty Years Work Among Them. New York, 1872.

Caroll, Betty Boyd. Italian Repatriation from the United States, 1900-1914. New York, 1973.

Carosso, Vincent. The California Wine Industry. Berkeley, 1951.

Carpenter, Niles. Immigrants and Their Children. Washington, D.C., 1927.

Carr, John Foster. The Italian Immigrant Looks at the Future. New York, 1918.

Chapin, Robert Coit. The Standard of Living Among Workingmen's Families in New York City. New York, 1909.

Child, Irwin. Italian or American: The Second Generation in Conflict. New Haven, 1943.

Claghorn, Kate H. The Immigrants' Day in Court. New York, 1923.

Clark, Francis Edward. Our Italian Fellow Citizens in Their Old Homes and Their New. Boston, 1919.

Cole, Donald B. Immigrant City, Lawrence, Massachusetts, 1845-1921. Chapel Hill, 1963.

Cordasco, Francesco. Italians in the U.S.: A Bibliography of Reports, Texts, Critical Studies and Related Materials. New York, 1972.

_____. The Italian American Experience: An Annotated and Classified Bibliographical Guide With Selected Publications of the Casa Italiana Educational Bureau. New York, 1974.

_____. (ed.). The Italian Community and Its Language in the United States: The Annual Reports of the Italian Teachers Association. Totowa, New Jersey, 1975.

_____. (ed.). Studies in Italian American Social History: Essays in Honor of Leonard Covello. Totowa, New Jersey, 1975.

_____ and Eugene Bucchioni. The Italians: Social Backgrounds of an American Group. Clifton, New Jersey, 1974.

Coulter, Charles W. The Italians of Cleveland. Cleveland, 1919.

Covello, Leonard. The Social Background of the Italo-American School Child: A Study of the Southern Italian Family Mores and Their Effect on the School Situation in Italy and America. Leiden, 1967.

De Conde, Alexander. Half Bitter, Half Sweet: An Excursion into Italian American History. New York, 1971.

Dickinson, Robert E. The Population Problem of Southern Italy: An Essay in Social Geography. Syracuse, 1955.

Diggins, John P. Mussolini and Fascism: The View from America. Princeton, 1972.

Douglas, David W. Influence of the Southern Italian in American Society. New York, 1915.

Ehrmann, Herbert B. The Case That Will Not Die: Commonwealth v. Sacco and Vanzetti. Boston, 1969.

Erickson, Charlotte. American Industry and the European Immigrant, 1860-1885. Cambridge, Massachusetts, 1957.

Ernst, Robert, Immigrant Life in New York City, 1825-1863. New York, 1949.

Federal Writers' Project. The Italians of New York. New York, 1938.

Felici, Icilio. Father to the Immigrants: The Life of John Baptist Scalabrini. New York, 1955.

Fermi, Laura. Illustrious Immigrants: The Intellectual Migration from Europe, 1930-1941. Chicago, 1968.

Fleming, Donald and Bernard Bailyn. (eds.). The Intellectual Migration: Europe and America, 1930-1960. Cambridge, Massachusetts, 1968.

Foerster, Robert F. The Italian Emigration of Our Time. Cambridge, Massachusetts, 1919.

Francesconi, Mario. Immigrants and Priests: The Scalabrinian Fathers in North America, 1888-1895. New York, 1974.

Gage, Nicholas. The Mafia is not an Equal Opportunity Employer. New York, 1972.

Gambino, Richard. Blood of My Blood: The Dilemma of the Italian Americans. New York, 1974.

Gans, Herbert J. The Urban Villagers: Group and Class in the Life of Italian Americans. New York, 1962.

Garlick, Jr., Richard C. et al. Italy and Italians in Washington's Time. New York, 1933.

_____. Philip Mazzei, Friend of Jefferson: His Life and Letters. Baltimore, 1933.

Garrett, Charles. The La Guardia Years: Machine and Reform Politics in New York City. New Brunswick, New Jersey, 1961.

Gebhart, John C. The Growth and Development of Italian Children in New York City. New York, 1924.

Glanz, Rudolf. Jew and Italian: Historic Group Relations and the New Immigration, 1881-1924. New York, 1970.

Glazer, Nathan and Daniel P. Moynihan. Beyond the Melting Pot: The Negroes, Puerto Ricans, Jews, Italians, and Irish of New York City. Cambridge, Massachusetts, 1963.

Goggio. Emilio. Italians in American History. New York, 1930.

Green, Rose B. The Italian American Novel: A Document of the Interaction of Two Cultures. Rutherford, New Jersey, 1974.

Grossman, Ronald P. The Italians in America. Minneapolis, Minnesota, 1966.

Hess, Henner. Mafia and Mafiosi: The Structure of Power. Lexington, Massachusetts, 1973.

Higham, John. Strangers in the Land: Patterns of American Nativism, 1860-1925. New York, 1960.

Hughes, H. Stuart. The United States and Italy. Cambridge, Massachusetts, 1965.

Hutchinson, Edward P. Immigrants and Their Children, 1850-1950. New York, 1956.

Iorizzo, Luciano J. and Salvatore Mondello. The Italian Americans. New York, 1971.

James, Marquis and Bessie R. Biography of a Bank: The Story of Bank of America. New York, 1954.

Jones, Maldwyn Allen. American Immigration. Chicago, 1960.

Joughin, G. Louis and Edmund M. Morgan. The Legacy of Sacco and Vanzetti. New York, 1948.

Kessner, Thomas. The Golden Door: Italian and Jewish Mobility in New York City, 1880-1915. New York, 1977.

Kobler, John. Capone, The Life and World of Al Capone. New York, 1971.

Krickus, Richard. Pursuing the American Dream: White Ethnics and the New Populism. New York, 1976.

Landesco, John. Organized Crime in Chicago. Chicago, 1929.

La Piana, George. The Italians in Milwaukee, Wisconsin. Milwaukee, 1915.

Levi, Carlo. Christ Stopped at Eboli. New York, 1947.

Linkh, Richard M. American Catholicism and European Immigrants, 1900-1924. New York, 1974.

Livi Bacci, Massimo. L'Immigrazione e L'Assimilazione Degli Italiani Negli Stati Uniti, Secondo Le Statistiche Demografiche Americane. Milan, 1961. (This is such a valuable book that even though it is in Italian, it still must be listed. It is easily found throughout the U.S. and its mathematical language makes it understandable to most students irregardless of language background.)

Lockwood, Frank C. With Padre Kino on the Trail. Tucson, 1934.

Lombardo, Anthony. The Italians in America. Chicago, 1973.

Lopreato, Joseph. Italian Americans. New York, 1970.

_____. Peasants No More. San Francisco, 1967.

Lord, Eliot, et al. The Italian in America. New York, 1905.

Maas, Peter. The Valachi Papers. New York, 1968.

Mangano, Antonio. Italian Colonies in New York City. New York, 1904.

_____. Religious Work for Italians in America: A Handbook for Leaders in Missionary Work. New York, 1915.

_____. Sons of Italy: A Social and Religious Study of Italians in America.
New York, 1917.

Mann, Arthur. La Guardia, A Fighter Against His Times, 1882-1933. Philadelphia,
1959.

Mariano, John Horace. Second Generation Italians in New York City. Boston, 1921.

_____. The Italian Contribution to American Society. Boston, 1921.

_____. The Italian Immigrant and Our Courts. Boston, 1925.

Marinacci, Barbara. They Came from Italy: The Stories of Famous Italian Americans.
New York, 1967.

Martin, Raymond. Revolt in the Mafia. New York, 1964.

Maynard, Theodore. Too Small a World: The Life of Francesca Cabrini. Milwaukee,
1945.

Meltzer, Milton. Bread and Roses: The Struggle of American Labor, 1865-1915. New
York, 1967.

Montgomery, Robert H. Sacco-Vanzetti: The Murder and the Myth. New York, 1960.

Moquin, Wayne and Charles Van Doren. (eds.). A Documentary History of the Italian
Americans. New York, 1974.

Morison, Samuel Eliot. Admiral of the Ocean Sea: A Life of Christopher Columbus.
Boston, 1942.

Murdock, Myrtle Cheney. Constantino Brumidi, Michelangelo of the United States
Capitol. Washington, D.C., 1965.

Murphy, Edmund Robert. Henry De Tonty: Fur Trader of the Mississippi. Baltimore,
1941.

Murray, Robert K. Red Scare: A Study in National Hysteria, 1919-1920. Minneapolis,
1955.

Musmanno, Michael A. The Story of Italians in America. New York, 1965.

Nelli, Humbert S. Italians in Chicago, 1880-1930: A Study in Ethnic Mobility. New
York, 1970.

_____. The Business of Crime: Italians and Syndicate Crime in the United
States. New York, 1976.

Nicosia, Francesco M. Italian Pioneers of California. San Francisco, 1960.

Novak, Michael. The Rise of the Unmeltable Ethnics: Politics and Culture in the
Seventies. New York, 1971.

Odencrantz, Louise C. Italian Women in Industry: A Study of Conditions in New York
City. New York, 1919.

Panunzio, Constantine M. Immigrant Crossroads. New York, 1927.

_____. The Immigrant Portrayed in Biography and Story: A Selected List with Notes. New York, 1925.

_____. The Soul of the Immigrant. New York, 1921.

Pellegrini, Angelo M. American by Choice. New York, 1956.

_____. Immigrant's Return. New York, 1951.

Peragallo, Olga. (ed.). Italian American Authors and Their Contribution to American Literature. New York, 1949.

Perilli, Giovanni. Colorado and the Italians in Colorado. Denver, 1922.

Pisani, Lawrence F. The Italian in America: A Social Study and History. New York, 1957.

Preston, William. Aliens and Dissenters: Federal Suppression of Radicals, 1903-1933. Cambridge, Massachusetts, 1963.

Puzo, Mario. The Fortunate Pilgrim. New York, 1964.

_____. The Godfather. New York, 1969.

Radin, Paul. The Italians of San Francisco. San Francisco, 1935.

Riis, Jacob A. Out of Mulberry Street. New York, 1898.

Rolle, Andrew F. The American Italians: Their History and Culture. Belmont, California, 1972.

_____. The Immigrant Upraised: Italian Adventurers and Colonists in an Expanding America. Norman, 1968.

Rose, Philip M. The Italians in America. New York, 1922.

Roselli, Bruno. Vigo: A Forgotten Builder of the American Republic. Boston, 1933.

_____. Italian Yesterday and Today: A History of Italian Teaching in the United States. Boston, 1935.

_____. Our Italian Immigrants: Their Racial Backgrounds. New York, 1927.

_____. The Italians in Colonial Florida. Jacksonville, 1940.

Rosenbaum, Gerald. Immigrant Workers: Their Impact on American Labor Radicalism. New York, 1973.

Russell, Francis. Tragedy in Dedham: The Story of the Sacco-Vanzetti Case. New York, 1962.

Salvemini, Gaetano. Italian Fascist Activities in the U.S. Washington, D.C., 1940.

Sartorio, Hnery Charles. Social and Religious Life of Italians in America. Boston, 1918.

Schiavo, Giovanni. Four Centuries of Italian American History. 2 vols. New York, 1952.

_____. Italian American History. New York, 1947.

_____. Philip Mazzei: One of America's Founding Fathers. New York, 1951.

_____. The Italians in America Before the Civil War. New York, 1934.

_____. The Italians in Chicago: A Story in Americanization. Chicago, 1928.

_____. The Italians in Missouri. New York, 1929.

_____. The Truth About the Mafia and Organized Crime in America. New York, 1962.

Seidman, Joel. The Needle Trades. New York, 1942.

Shriver, William Payne. The Story of Presbyterian Work with Italians. New York, 1946.

Smith, Denis Mack. A History of Sicily: Modern Sicily After 1713. New York, 1968.

_____. Italy: A Modern History. Ann Arbor, 1959.

Sondern, Frederic. Brotherhood of Evil, the Mafia. New York, 1959.

Stella, Antonio A. Some Aspects of Italian Immigration to the U.S.: Statistical Data Based Chiefly Upon the U.S. Census and Other Official Publications. New York, 1924.

_____. The Effects of Urban Congestion on Italian Women and Children. New York, 1908.

Tait, Joseph W. Some Aspects of the Effects of the Dominant American Culture Upon Children of Italian Born Parents. New York, 1942.

Talese, Gay. Honor Thy Father. New York, 1971.

Teresa, Vincent. My Life in the Mafia. New York, 1973.

Tomasi, Lydio F. The Italian American Family: The Southern Italian American Family's Process of Adjustment to an Urban America. New York, 1972.

_____. (ed.). The Italian in America: The Progressive View, 1891-1914. New York, 1972.

Tomasi, Silvano M. An Overview of Current Efforts and Studies in the Field of Italian Immigration. New York, 1968.

_____. The Italians in America. New York, 1971.

_____. Piety and Power: The Role of the Italian Parishes in the New York Metropolitan Area. New York, 1975.

_____ and M. H. Engel. (eds.). The Italian Experience in the United States. New York, 1970.

Torrielli, Andrew J. Italian Opinion on America as Revealed by Italian Travelers, 1850-1900. Cambridge, Massachusetts, 1941.

Trease, Geoffrey. The Italian Story: From the Etruscans to Modern Times. New York, 1963.

Trisco, Robert F. The Holy See and the Nascent Church in the Middle Western States, 1826-1850. Rome, 1964.

U.S. Immigration Commission. The Children of Immigrants in Schools. 5 vols. Washington, D.C., 1911.

_____. Reports. 41 vols. Washington, D.C., 1911.

Van Kleeck, Mary. Artificial Flower Makers. New York, 1913.

Velikonja, Joseph. Italians in the U.S.: A Bibliography. Peoria, Illinois, 1963.

Ware, Caroline F. Greenwich Village, 1920-1930: A Comment on American Civilization in the Post-War Years. New York, 1935.

Wheeler, Thomas C. The Immigrant Experience: The Anguish of Becoming an American. New York, 1971.

Whyte, William F. Street Corner Society: The Social Structure of an Italian Slum. Chicago, 1943.

Williams, Phyllis H. South Italian Folkways in Europe and America. New Haven, 1938.

Willis, F. Roy. Italy Chooses Europe. New York, 1971.

Work Progress Administration. The Italians of Omaha. Omaha, 1941.

Wyllys, Rufus Kay. Pioneer Padre: The Life and Times of Eusebio Kino. Dallas, Texas, 1935.

Zinn, Howard. La Guardia in Congress. Ithaca, New York, 1959.

Articles

"A Selected List of Bibliographical References and Records of the Italians in the U.S.," Italian Library of Information. Series 1, Number 5 (August 1958).

Baily, Samuel L. "The Italians and Organized Labor in the United States and Argentina: 1800-1910," The International Migration Review, I (Summer 1967), 56-66.

_____. "The Italians and the Development of Organized Labor in Argentina, Brazil, and the United States, 1880-1914," Journal of Social History, III (Winter 1969), 123-134.

Barbaro, Fred. "Ethnic Affirmation, Affirmative Action, and the Italian Americans," Italian Americana, I, 1 (Autumn 1974), 41-58.

Bell, Daniel. "Crime as an American Way of Life: A Queer Ladder of Social Mobility," The End of Ideology. New York, 1962.

Boissevain, Jeremy. "Poverty and Politics in a Sicilian Agro-Town," International Archives of Ethnography, 50, pt. 2 (1966).

Brandfon, Robert L. "The End of Immigration to the Cotton Fields," Mississippi Valley Historical Review, L (March 1964), 591-611.

Browne, Henry J. "The Italian Problem in the Catholic Church of the United States, 1880-1900," Historical Records and Studies, XXXV (1946), 46-75.

Campisi, Paul J. "Ethnic Family Patterns: The Italian Family in the United States," The American Journal of Sociology, LIII (May 1948), 443-449.

Castiglione, G. E. Di Palma. "Italian Immigration into the United States, 1901-1904," American Journal of Sociology, II (September 1905), 183-206.

Cerase, Francesco P. "Expectations and Reality: A Case Study of Return Migration from the United States to Southern Italy," The International Migration Review, VIII, 26 (Summer 1974), 245-262.

_____. "A Study of Italian Migrants Returning from the U.S.A.," The International Migration Review, I, 3 (Summer 1967), 67-74.

Cometti, Elizabeth. "Trends in Italian Migration," Western Political Quarterly, XI (December 1958), 820-834.

Cordasco, F. "The Children of Immigrants in Schools: Historical Analogues of Educational Deprivation," The Journal of Negro Education, XLII (Winter 1973).

_____. "The Children of Columbus: The New Italian American Ethnic Historiography," Phylon (September 1973).

Corsi, Edward. "Italian Immigrants and Their Children," Annals of the American Academy of Political and Social Science, CCXXIII (September 1942), 100-106.

Covello, Leonard. "A High School and Its Immigrant Community: A Challenge and an Opportunity," Journal of Educational Sociology, IX (February 1936), 333-346.

Coxe, John E. "The New Orleans Mafia Incident," Louisiana Historical Quarterly, XX (October 1937), 1067-1110.

Dickinson, Joan Y. "Aspects of Italian Immigration to Philadelphia," Pennsylvania Magazine of History and Biography, XL (October 1966), 445-465.

Diggins, John P. "American Catholics and Italian Fascism," Journal of Contemporary History, II (October 1967), 51-68.

_____. "Mussolini and America: Hero-Worship Charisma and the 'Vulgar Talent,'" The Historian, XXVIII (August 1966), 559-585.

_____. "The Italo-American Anti-Fascist Opposition," Journal of Modern History, LIV (December 1967), 579-598.

Dore, Grazia, "Some Social and Historical Aspects of Italian Emigration to America," Journal of Social History, II, 2 (Winter 1968), 95-122.

Duff, John B. "The Italians," The Immigrants Influence on Wilson's Peace Policies. Edited by Joseph P. O'Grady. Lexington, Kentucky, 1967.

Femminella, Francis X. "The Impact of Italian Migration and American Catholicism," American Catholic Sociological Review, XXII (Fall 1961), 233-241.

Feton, Edwin. "Italian Immigrants in the Stoneworkers' Union," Labor History, III (Spring 1962), 188-207.

_____. "Italians in the Labor Movement," Pennsylvania History, XXVI (April 1959), 133-148.

Foerster, Robert F. "A Statistical Survey of Italian Emigration," Quarterly Journal of Economics, XXIII (November 1908), 66-103.

Gambino, Richard. "Twenty Million Italian Americans Can't Be Wrong," New York Times Magazine, April 30, 1972.

Gans, Herbert J. "Some Comments on the History of Italian Migration and on the Nature of Historical Research," International Migration Review, I (Summer 1967), 5-9.

Gilkey, George R. "The United States and Italy: Migration and Repatriation," The Journal of Developing Areas, II (October 1967), 23-36.

Goggio, Emilio. "Italian Educators in Early American Days," Atlantica, XI (June 1931), 255-256, 281.

Hale, Edward Everett, "The Padrone Question," Review of Reviews, August 1894, pp. 192-193.

Heiss, Jerold. "Sources of Satisfaction and Assimilation Among Italian Immigrants," Human Relations, XIX (May 1966), 165-177.

Hewes, Leslie. "Tontitown: Ozark Vineyard Center," Economic Geography, XXIX (April 1953), 125-143.

Ianni, Francis A. J. "Residential and Occupational Mobility as Indices of the Acculturation of an Ethnic Group," Social Forces, XXXVI (October 1957), 65-72.

_____. "The Mafia and the Web of Kinship," Public Interest (Winter 1971), 78-100.

Iorizzo, Luciano J. "The Padrone and Immigrant Distribution," in The Italian Experience in the United States. Edited by S. M. Tomasi and M. H. Engels. New York, 1970.

_____, and Salvatore Mondello, "Origins of Italian American Criminality: From New Orleans Through Prohibition," Italian Americana, I, 2 (Spring 1975), 217-236.

Juliani, Richard N. "The Origin and Development of the Italian Community in Philadelphia," in The Ethnic Experience in Pennsylvania. Edited by John E. Bodnar. Cranbury, New Jersey, 1973. Pp. 233-262.

Karlin, Jules A. "New Orleans Lynchings of 1891 and the American Press," Louisiana Historical Quarterly, XXIV (January 1941), 187-203.

_____. "The Italo-American Incident of 1891 and the Road to Reunion," Journal of Southern History, VIII (May 1942), 242-246.

Kendall, J. S. "Who Killa de Chief?" Louisiana Historical Quarterly, XXII (January 1939), 492-530.

Koren, John. "The Padrone System and Padrone Banks," Bulletin of the Department of Labor, 9. Washington, D.C., 1897. Pp. 113-129.

Lancaster, Clay. "Italianism in American Architecture Before 1860," American Quarterly, IV (Summer, 1952), 127-148.

Levi, Carlo. "Italy's Myth of America," Life, XXIII (July 1947), 84-85.

Lipari, Marie. "The Padrone System," Italy-American Monthly, II (April 1935), 4-10.

Marraro, Howard R. "Interpretation of Italy and the Italians in Eighteenth Century America," Italica, XXV, I (1948), 59-81.

_____. "Italian Music and Actors in America During the Eighteenth Century," Italica, XXIII (June 1946), 103-117.

_____. "Philip Mazzei on American Political, Social, and Economic Problems," The Journal of Southern History, XV (August 1949), 354-378.

_____. "Pioneer Italian Teachers of Italian in the United States," The Modern Language Journal, XXVIII (November 1944), 555-582.

_____. "The Teaching of Italian in America in the Eighteenth Century," The Modern Language Teacher, XXV (November 1940), 120-125.

McBride, Paul. "The Italian Americans and the Catholic Church: Old and New Perspectives--A Review Essay," Italian Americana, I, 2 (Spring 1975), 265-279.

Meade, Emily F. "Italian Immigration into the South," South Atlantic Quarterly, IV (July 1905), 217-223.

_____. "The Italians on the Land," United States Bureau of Labor Bulletin, LXX, Washington, D.C., 1907.

Mondello, Salvatore. "Protestant Proselytism Among the Italians in the U.S.A. as Reported in American Magazines," Social Sciences, XLI (April 1966), 84-90.

Monticelli, Giuseppe Lucrezio. "Italian Emigration: Basic Characteristics and Trends with Special Reference to the Last Twenty Years," International Migration Review, I, 3 (Summer 1967), 10-24.

Nelli, Humbert S. "Italians and Crime in Chicago: The Formative Years, 1890-1920," The American Journal of Sociology, LXXIV (January 1969), 373-391.

_____. "Italians in Urban America: A Study in Ethnic Adjustment," The International Migration Review, I (Summer 1967), 38-55.

_____. "The Italian Padrone System in the United States," Labor History, V (Spring 1964), 153-167.

Owens, M. L. "Frances Xavier Cabrini," Colorado Magazine, XXII (July 1945), 171-178.

Pecorini, Alberto. "The Italian as an Agricultural Laborer," Annals of the American Academy of Political and Social Sciences, XXXIII (1909), pp. 380-390.

Pileggi, Nicholas. "Little Italy: Study of an Italian Ghetto," New York, I (August 12, 1968), 14-23.

Ra___, Anna Maria. "Italian Migration Movements from 1876-1926," International Migrations, II (1931), 440-470.

Riis, Jacob A. "The Italian in New York," in How the Other Half Lives: Studies Among the Tenements of New York. New York, 1890.

Rodgers, A. "Migration and Industrial Development: The Southern Italian Experience," Southern Geography, XLVI (April 1970), 111-135.

Rolle, Andrew F. "Italy in California," The Pacific Spectator, IX (Autumn 1955), 408-419.

_____. "The Italian Moves Westward," Montana: The Magazine of Western History, XVI (Winter 1966), 13-24.

Rosenwalke, Ira. "Two Generations of Italians in America: Their Fertility Experience," The International Migration Review, VII, 23 (Fall 1973), 271-280.

Russo, Nicholas John. "Three Generations of Italians in New York City : Their Religious Acculturation," The International Migration Review, III, 8 (Spring 1969), 3-17.

Sassone, Thommaso. "Italy's Criminals in the United States," Current History, XV (October 1921), 23-31.

Scalia, Eugene S. "Figures of the Risorgimento in America," Italica, XLII (December 1965), 311-357.

Scarpaci, Jean Ann. "Immigrants in the New South: Italians in Louisiana's Sugar Parishes, 1880-1910," Labor History (Summer 1974), 183-197.

Schuyler, Eugene. "Italian Immigration into the United States," Political Science Quarterly, IV (September 1889), 480-495.

Sheridan, Frank J. "Italian, Slavic, and Hungarian Unskilled Immigrant Laborers in the United States," Bulletin of the Bureau of Labor, XV, 72, Washington, D.C., 1907. Pp. 403-486.

Tomasi, Silvano M. "The Ethnic Church and the Integration of Italian Immigrants in the United States," in The Italian Experience in the United States, New York, 1970.

Tortosa, V.R. "Italian Americans, Their Swing to the G.O.P.," The Nation, CLXXVII (October 24, 1953), 330-332.

Tosti, Gustavo. "Italy's Attitude Toward Her Emigrants," North American Review, CLXXX (May 1905), 720-726.

Vecoli, Rudolph J. "Contadini in Chicago: A Critique of the Uprooted," Journal of American History, LIV (December 1964), 404-417.

_____. "Prelates and Peasants: Italian Immigrants and the Catholic Church, Journal of Social History, II (Spring 1969), 217-268.

Velikonja, Joseph. "Italian Immigrants in the United States in the Mid-Sixties," The International Migration Review, I, 3 (Summer 1967), 25-37.